GRILL BY THE BOOK

Chicken and Other Poultry

By the Editors of Sunset Books

with special contributions by

Jerry Anne Di Vecchio
and
Betty Hughes

Sunset Books Inc.
Menlo Park, California

President & Publisher:
Susan J. Maruyama

Director, Sales & Marketing:
Richard A. Smeby

Director, New Business:
Kenneth Winchester

Editorial Director:
Bob Doyle

Marketing & Creative Services Manager:
Guy C. Joy

Production Director:
Lory Day

EDITORIAL STAFF FOR CHICKEN AND OTHER POULTRY

Coordinating Editor:
Lynne Gilberg

Research & Text:
Paula Smith Freschet

Consulting Editor:
Betty Hughes, Director, Consumer Affairs, Weber-Stephen Products Co.

Contributing Editors:
Sandra Cameron
Barbara Sause
Cynthia Scheer

Copy Editor:
Fran Feldman

Editorial Assistant:
Jody Mitori

Photography:
Chris Shorten

Food Stylists:
Heidi Gintner
Susan Massey
Dianne Torrie
Sue White

Food Styling Assistant:
Andrea Lucich

Prop Stylist:
Laura Ferguson

Design:
Don Komai, Watermark Design

Page Layout:
Dayna Goforth

Recipe Testers:
Susan Block
Dorothy Decker
Barbara Gobar
Aileen Russell
Jean Strain
Linda Tebben

SUNSET PUBLISHING CORPORATION

Chairman:
Jim Nelson

President & Chief Executive Officer:
Stephen J. Seabolt

Chief Financial Officer:
James E. Mitchell

Publisher, Sunset Magazine:
Anthony P. Glaves

Director of Finance:
Larry Diamond

Circulation Director:
Robert I. Gursha

Vice President, Manufacturing:
Lorinda Reichert

Editor, Sunset Magazine:
William Marken

Senior Editor, Food & Entertaining:
Jerry Anne Di Vecchio

For more information on *Grill by the Book* or any other Sunset book, call 1-800-526-5111.

A word about our nutritional data

For our recipes, we provide a nutritional analysis stating calorie count; percentage of calories from fat; grams of total fat and saturated fat; milligrams of cholesterol and sodium; grams of carbohydrates, fiber, and protein; and milligrams of calcium and iron. Generally, the analysis applies to a single serving, based on the number of servings given for each recipe and the amount of each ingredient. If a range is given for the number of servings and/or the amount of an ingredient, the analysis is based on the average of the figures given.

The nutritional analysis does not include optional ingredients or those for which no specific amount is stated. If an ingredient is listed with a substitution, the information was calculated using the first choice.

Contents

The Art of Grilling

Recipes

Index

Special Features

The Art of Grilling

Some folks say opposites attract, and I suppose that's how it was when Weber met Sunset. Weber is a Chicago-area company with a long tradition of forming steel into very durable barbecue grills. Sunset is a San Francisco-area company with a long tradition of forming words and photographs into informative and entertaining publications.

Weber's roots are in the Midwest, and I guess that means we really appreciate a good, thick steak and meaty ribs from the heartland. Sunset's roots are in California, where fresh Pacific seafood and an almost infinite variety of vegetables abound.

Now, even if opposites attract they must have something in common for a long-term relationship to develop.

You see, at Weber we believe you ought to buy one of our products and be pleasantly surprised that it exceeds your expectations. Sunset thinks the same way. When they write a recipe, the amount of testing they do to make sure it'll come out just so is mind-boggling.

About a year ago, Weber decided to produce a series of cookbooks to help backyard chefs have more fun with their grills. Sunset was considering a similar project. So, when we shared our mutual desire to write a series of simply great barbecue cookbooks, we decided we could make them even better if we formed a partnership.

We believe that this terrific cookbook will help you have fun with your grill, but if you have any suggestions for improvements, simply give us a call at the following number: (800) 446-1071. Your comments will help us get better at what we do, and we want to make sure you're totally satisfied with our products.

Mike Kempster

Michael Kempster, Sr.
Executive Vice President
Weber-Stephen Products Co.

A Range of Grill Options

Today's Weber® Grills come in a range of sizes, models, and prices, that offer backyard chefs a myriad of options. Before you purchase a grill, however, it's important to consider your cooking objectives. The grills described below offer a variety of convenient features that may be important to you.

No matter which Weber® model you choose, however, it's going to be a covered grill. The lid gives you the flexibility of using either the Direct or Indirect Methods of cooking. It also allows you to utilize more heat, reduces the amount of cooking time, and virtually eliminates flare-ups.

Weber® One-Touch® Charcoal Kettle

With the Weber® One-Touch® Kettle, one lever opens the vents to create the natural convection heat that helps seal in juices and flavor. The same lever also simplifies ash removal. Flip-up sides on the hinged cooking grate make it easy to add charcoal briquets while food cooks.

The kettle is available in two diameters: 18½ inches (47 cm) or 22½ inches (57 cm). Both offer plenty of cooking space.

Weber® Performer® Grill with Touch-N-Go™ Gas Ignition System

The ultimate ease in charcoal barbecuing begins with the exclusive gas ignition system on this grill, which makes quick work of lighting charcoal briquets. All you do is push a button. A high-capacity ash catcher makes cleaning easy, too. The large charcoal storage container keeps charcoal dry.

This model also has the Dual-Purpose Thermometer, the Tuck-Away™ Lid Holder, and Char-Basket™ Fuel Holders.

Weber®, Smokey Joe®, and Go-Anywhere® Grills

Smaller in size than the other Weber® grills, these transportable tabletop models cook the same way as their larger counterparts. They are available in charcoal and gas models.

Weber® Genesis® 3000 Series Gas Barbecue

A convenient alternative to cooking with charcoal, this grill features specially angled Flavorizer® Bars that distribute the heat evenly and vaporize the drippings to create barbecue flavor without flare-ups. Stainless steel burners run the length of the cooking box, offering controlled, even cooking and energy efficiency.

This grill has 635 square inches (4,097 square cm) of cooking area and warming racks. Its durable porcelain-enameled cooking grate is easy to clean.

Other features include the Dual-Purpose Thermometer, weather-resistant wood work surfaces, and an easy-to-read fuel scale. Available in liquid propane and natural gas models.

The Direct Method in a Charcoal Kettle

This grilling technique is best for relatively thin pieces of food that cook in less than 25 minutes; boneless chicken breasts, turkey tenderloins, and turkey breast slices fall in this category. Direct cooking is also used for steaks, chops, burgers, fish fillets and steaks, and shellfish. The food is placed directly over the hot coals.

To prepare the grill, open all of the vents and spread charcoal briquets in a single solid layer that fills the charcoal grate. Next, mound the briquets in a pyramid-shaped pile and ignite them, keeping the lid off. When the briquets are lightly coated with gray ash (25 to 30 minutes), use long-handled tongs to spread them into a single layer again. Set the cooking grate in place and arrange the food on the grate. Place the lid on the grill, leaving all vents open, and grill as directed in your recipe, turning the food once halfway through the cooking time.

The Direct Method in a Gas Barbecue

With gas grills, use of the Direct Method is limited to preheating and searing; most of the actual cooking is done by the Indirect Method.

To preheat the grill, open the lid and check that all burner control knobs are turned to OFF and the fuel scale reads more than "E." Turn on the gas at the source. Light with the igniter switch or, if necessary, a match (see the manufacturer's directions). Check through the viewing port to be sure the burner is lit. Close the lid, turn all burners to HIGH, and preheat 10 to 15 minutes to bring the grill to 500°–550°F (260°–288°C). Then adjust the heat controls as the recipe directs and proceed to cook the food. For searing techniques, see the box at right.

Searing

Searing cut-up poultry helps keep the meat moist by sealing in its juices. The hot fat that drips from the poultry creates smoke that gives the grilled foods their distinctive barbecue flavor. (Notes with the recipes throughout this book will indicate when searing is recommended.)

- ***To sear poultry in a gas barbecue**, first trim off any excess at. Preheat the grill as described at left, then arrange the pieces, skin sides down, on the cooking grate directly over the heat source and place the lid on the grill. Quickly brown the surfaces of the meat for about 2 minutes. (If excessive flaring occurs, turn the center burner to OFF until it subsides and then turn it to MEDIUM or LOW to complete searing.)*
  Turn the meat, placing it in the center of the cooking grate, and complete grilling by the Indirect Method over MEDIUM heat.

- ***To sear poultry in a charcoal kettle** that is set up for Indirect cooking, place the cut-up pieces, skin side down, at the outer edges of the cooking grate over the hot coals and sear as directed above. Turn the meat, placing it in the center of the cooking grate, and complete grilling by the Indirect Method as directed in the recipe.*

Indirect Cooking in a Charcoal Kettle

Use this method for whole birds and cut-up poultry that need to cook for more than 25 minutes at lower temperatures. This technique will also be used for roasts, ribs, and whole fish. The food is not turned, and the grill must be kept covered, since every time you open the lid, heat escapes and the cooking time increases.

To set up the grill for the Indirect Method, open all vents. Position Char-Basket™ Fuel Holders or charcoal rails on either side of the charcoal grate as close as possible to the outside edges. Divide the charcoal briquets evenly and place them in the holders (see the chart below for the number to use). Ignite the briquets and, keeping the lid off, let them burn until lightly covered with gray ash (25 to 30 minutes). If necessary, use long-handled tongs to rearrange briquets so the heat will be even.

Place a foil drip pan on the charcoal grate between the baskets of coals. Put the cooking grate in place, positioning the hinged sides of the grate over the briquets so that more can be added if necessary. Arrange the food in the center of the cooking grate. Place the lid on the grill, leaving all vents open, and grill as directed. If the food is to cook for more than an hour, add briquets as indicated on the chart.

Indirect Cooking in a Gas Barbecue

Except when you are searing, the Indirect Method is always the best approach to cooking on a gas grill. Turn the food only if you are directed to do so in the recipe. The grill must be kept covered or you will have to increase the cooking time. Let foods grill for the minimum time specified in the recipe before checking for doneness.

When using the Indirect Method, preheat as directed for the Direct Method (facing page). Arrange the food in the center of the cooking grate and place the lid on the grill. For three-burner grills, set the front and back burners to MEDIUM and the center burner to OFF; for two-burner grills, turn the front and back burners to MEDIUM.

If you have another brand of grill, check your owner's manual for Indirect cooking instructions.

Quick Smoke Flavoring

When you use a covered barbecue grill, wood chips or chunks placed beneath the cooking grate can add a delicate smoked flavor. Chips are ideal for foods with shorter cooking times; chunks are best for foods that take longer. The best woods for poultry are alder, apple, cherry, grapevine, hickory, mesquite, and oak. You may also want to experiment with orange peels, dried corn cobs, dried fennel stocks, garlic, or woody perennial fresh herbs.

Start by soaking the wood chips or chunks in water—30 minutes for chips, one hour for chunks.

In a charcoal grill, scatter a handful or two of the wet chips right over the hot coals. With a gas grill, turn the heat to HIGH and place the chips with a little bit of water in a small foil pan directly on the heat source in the left front corner of the grill. Used as directed, a Weber® Steam-N-Chips™ Smoker makes such quick smoking a snap. Preheat the barbecue as directed and cook by the Indirect Method on MEDIUM heat.

When the wood starts smoking, begin grilling, and keep the lid on. Add more soaked chips when you no longer see smoke exiting the vents. Remember, a little smoke goes a long way—you want the flavor to complement, not overpower, the food's natural taste.

The Right Amount of Charcoal for Indirect Cooking

Diameter of grill in inches	Briquets needed on each side for first hour	Number of briquets to add to each side every hour
26 ¾" (68 cm)	30	9
22 ½" (57 cm)	25	8
18 ½" (47 cm)	16	5

Fuels & Fire Starters

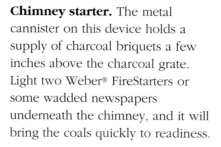

Charcoal briquets. Long the outdoor chef's favorite fuel, charcoal briquets are manufactured from pulverized charcoal and additives that make them easy to light. Once ignited, briquets provide good even heat, but the various brands differ somewhat in composition and density. Top-quality brands burn longer and more evenly. Store briquets in a dry place.

Self-starting briquets. Impregnated with a liquid starter, these briquets ignite with a match and heat up quickly. *Do not add self-starting briquets to an existing hot fire*—the fuel in them burns off slowly and it can spoil the flavor of the food. Always use regular briquets when additional charcoal is needed.

Liquid starter. If you use a liquid starter, be sure it's a product intended for charcoal, and follow the manufacturer's instructions closely. Let the starter soak into the coals for a few minutes; then ignite in several places. *Never* pour liquid starter on hot coals—this can cause a dangerous flare-up.

Solid starter. Solid starters such as Weber® FireStarters are safe, nontoxic, odorless cubes that light easily with a match and burn without further attention. Mound the briquets in a pyramid shape on top of the cubes, leaving a corner of the cubes exposed. Ignite the cubes, and the coals will be ready in 25 to 30 minutes.

Chimney starter. The metal cannister on this device holds a supply of charcoal briquets a few inches above the charcoal grate. Light two Weber® FireStarters or some wadded newspapers underneath the chimney, and it will bring the coals quickly to readiness.

Electric starter. Comprised of a large heating element, a handle, and an electrical cord, this device nestles in a bed of unlit briquets and ignites them when the cord is connected. After 10 minutes, remove the starter (if you leave it in too long, the heating element will burn out).

Liquid propane and natural gas. Gas barbecues use either liquid propane or natural gas as fuel. Liquid propane is stored in a refillable tank mounted on the barbecue grill. Expect 20 to 30 hours of use from a tank. Natural gas is piped to a grill through a permanent hookup to a gas line. *Note:* Never use one kind of fuel in a barbecue grill designed for the other.

Fire Safety

Follow the manufacturer's instructions carefully and heed the rules below to ensure safety while you grill.

■ *Never leave a hot grill unattended. Keep children and pets at a safe distance.*

■ *Never use a charcoal or gas grill indoors or in a closed garage or enclosed patio.*

■ *Do not use gasoline or other highly volatile fluids as charcoal lighters.*

■ *Do not add liquid starter to hot—or even warm—coals.*

■ *Place your grill in an open, level area away from the house, wood railings, trees, bushes, or other combustible surfaces.*

■ *Do not attempt to barbecue in high winds.*

■ *Wear an insulated, fire-retardant barbecue mitt and use long-handled tools designed for grilling. Do not wear clothing with loose, flowing sleeves.*

Grilling Guide for Poultry

Type of Poultry	Weight or Thickness	Approximate Cooking Time
BONELESS CHICKEN & TURKEY		

Place food on cooking grate, using Direct Method for a charcoal grill, Indirect Method/Medium Heat for a gas grill. Cook for time given in chart, based on medium-well 170°F (77°C), or until meat in thickest part is no longer pink; turn once halfway through cooking time.

Type of Poultry	Weight or Thickness	Approximate Cooking Time
Chicken		
Breasts	4–5 oz (115–140 g) *each*	10 minutes
Breast cubes	1 inch (2.5 cm)	10–12 minutes
Turkey		
Tenderloins	About 6 oz (170 g) *each*	10–12 minutes
Breast slices	¼ inch (6 mm) thick	3–5 minutes
Breast cubes	1 inch (2.5 cm)	12–15 minutes

BONE-IN PIECES & WHOLE BIRDS

Place food on cooking grate, using Indirect Method for a charcoal grill, Indirect Method/Medium Heat for a gas grill. Cook *bone-in pieces,* bone side down, for time given in chart or until no longer pink near bone; sear first, if desired. Cook *whole birds,* breast side up, for time given in chart or until an instant-read thermometer inserted in thickest part of thigh (not touching bone) registers 180°F (82°C); begin checking doneness 30 minutes before minimum cooking time.

Type of Poultry	Weight or Thickness	Approximate Cooking Time
Chicken		
Whole	3½–4 lbs (1.6–1.8 kg)	1–1½ hours
Halves	1½–1¾ lbs (680–795 g) *each*	50–60 minutes
Breast halves	About 8 oz (230 g) *each*	30–35 minutes
Drumsticks, thighs	4–6 oz (115–170 g) *each*	35–45 minutes
Wings	About 3 oz (85 g) *each*	30 minutes
Rock Cornish Game Hens		
Whole	1–1½ lbs (455–680 g)	45–60 minutes
Halves	8–12 oz (230–340 g) *each*	35–45 minutes
Turkey		
Whole	10–13 lbs (4.5–5.9 kg)	1½–2¼ hours
	14–23 lbs (6.4–10.4 kg)	2½–3½ hours
Breast halves	3–3½ lbs (1.35–1.6 kg) *each*	1–1½ hours
Drumsticks, thighs	1–1½ lbs (455–680 g) *each*	55–65 minutes
Duck		
Whole	4–5 lbs (1.8–2.3 kg)	1½–2 hours
Farm-raised, halves	12–16 oz (340–455 g) *each*	30–35 minutes
Pheasant		
Whole	2–2½ lbs (905 g–1.15 kg)	40–45 minutes

Buying and Storing Poultry

How Much to Buy

From a strictly nutritional standpoint, the recommended serving of cooked poultry is 3 ounces (85 g); about 4 ounces (115 g) of lean, boneless, uncooked poultry will yield a serving that size. Many people enjoy eating more than that, however.

In general, figure the number of servings by a bird's weight (bone-in). With whole chickens, turkeys, and Rock Cornish game hens, buy about 1 pound (455 g) per serving. For duck expect 2 or 3 servings from a 4- to 5-pound (1.8- to 2.3-kg) bird. A 1½-pound (680-g) pheasant will only serve one, but a 3-pound (1.35-kg) bird should provide about 3 servings.

Purchasing Poultry

Make sure fresh poultry has been kept refrigerated, not held at room temperature. If it's prepackaged, select trays with little or no liquid on the bottom. Good-quality whole birds have smooth, tight skin and plump breasts and drumsticks. Turkey should have cream-colored skin.

Avoid torn packages of frozen poultry—if the bird hasn't been kept airtight, it has probably lost moisture. Packages containing frozen liquid indicate that the meat at some point was partially thawed and then refrozen.

Storing Poultry

Cook fresh poultry within 2 days of purchase; otherwise, freeze it (see chart below for storage times).

To refrigerate poultry, leave it in the wrapping from the market to avoid introducing bacteria by repeated handling (if the wrapping is torn, replace it with wax paper, plastic wrap, or foil). Place the poultry in the coldest part of the refrigerator.

To freeze poultry, wrap it airtight in moistureproof freezer paper (wrap even prepackaged meat for extra insulation). Label the packages with the type of bird, the weight, and the date. Freeze at 0°F (–18°C). To freeze necks and giblets, place necks, hearts, and gizzards in one container and livers in another.

Thawing Poultry

Always fully defrost poultry before grilling. The safest way is to let it stand, well wrapped, in the refrigerator. Allow 12 to 16 hours for a whole chicken, and 4 to 9 hours for chicken parts, depending on size and number. For a whole turkey, allow 1 to 2 days for a 10- to 12- pound (4.5- to 5.5-kg) bird, 2 to 3 days for a 13- to 16-pound (5.9- to 7.3-kg) bird, 3 to 4 days for a 17- to 20-pounder (7.7- to 9.1-kg), and 4 to 5 days for a 21- to 23-pounder (9.6- to 10.4-kg). Turkey parts take 1 to 2 days. For a whole duck weighing 4 to 5 pounds (1.8 to 2.3-kg), allow 24 to 36 hours.

If you must thaw poultry quickly, enclose it in a watertight plastic bag and place in cold water; change the water often. To thaw poultry in a microwave oven, follow the manufacturer's instructions.

Do not thaw poultry in warm water or at room temperature. Bacteria that cause food poisoning can develop rapidly under these conditions.

Refrigerator & Freezer Storage Times for Poultry

Type of Poultry	Refrigerator storage at 36°–40°F (2°–4°C)	Freezer storage at 0°F (–18°C)
Chicken and turkey (whole)	1–2 days	12 months
Chicken and turkey pieces	1–2 days	9 months
Rock Cornish game hen	1–2 days	9 months
Duck and pheasant	1–2 days	6 months
Giblet	1–2 days	3–4 months

Cutting a Whole Chicken

Place the chicken breast side up, then pull a leg away from body and cut through the meat, exposing the joint. Bend the thigh down and sever. Repeat for the other leg.

Cut down to the joint between the thigh and the drumstick. Bend the pieces back to fully expose the joint, then sever.

Pull a wing away from the body. Cut through the skin and meat to expose the joint, then sever. Repeat to remove the other wing.

To remove the lower back, cut along the bottom ribs on each side of the breast to the backbone. Bend the back in half and cut to separate.

With the breast turned down, cut to the shoulder joints along the sides of the upper back. Bend the breast and back apart to expose the joints, then sever.

To halve the breast, cut through the thin membrane down to the keel bone (a dark spoon-shaped bone); then cut along one side of the bone and the cartilage.

Preparing a Whole Bird for the Grill

Remove the neck and giblets; rinse bird inside and out and pat dry. Twist the wing tips under the back.

Pull skin over the neck and body cavities and secure them with small metal skewers.

Bring the legs together and tie them with cotton string. If you're grilling a duck, prick the skin all over.

11

Boning a Whole Chicken Breast

Place the breast skin side down and run a sharp knife down its center to sever the thin membrane and expose the dark spoon-shaped keel bone and the white cartilage.

Placing one thumb on the tip end of the keel bone and the other at base of the rib cage, grasp the breast firmly in both hands. Bend it back until the keel bone breaks through.

Run a finger under the edge of the keel bone and cartilage, first loosening them, then grasp them firmly and pull them out. Discard the bone and cartilage.

Insert knife under the long first rib, rest the blade against the ribs, and scrape meat away. Sever shoulder joint; remove ribs and attached bone. Repeat for other side of breast.

Locate the wishbone with your fingers. Cutting close to bone, remove wishbone.

Lay breast flat on a cutting board and cut in half; remove white tendon from bottom of each half. Pull off skin, if desired.

Safety Guidelines for Poultry

All poultry is a potential host for dangerous organisms that can cause spoilage and food poisoning. To avoid problems, follow proper storage, cooking, and handling procedures. Practice these safety tips:

■ *Refrigerate poultry as soon as possible after purchase. Throw out any poultry that has an off odor or looks bad.*

■ *Never thaw poultry on the countertop at room temperature or in warm water. Thaw it in the refrigerator.*

■ *Thoroughly wash your hands, utensils, and work surfaces with hot, soapy water after handling raw poultry. To sanitize work surfaces and utensils, treat them with diluted chlorine bleach (2 to 3 teaspoons bleach per quart/950 liters water) and rinse well.*

■ *Cut raw and cooked poultry on a nonporous surface (such as acrylic) instead of on wood.*

■ *Use separate dishes for raw and cooked poultry.*

■ *Never let cooked poultry stand at room temperature for more than 2 hours.*

■ *The USDA recommendation is that ground poultry be cooked to 165°F (74°C) in center of patties or until no longer pink and the juices run clear.*

Butterflying & Skewering Whole Birds

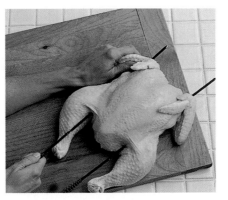

With poultry shears or a knife, split the bird lengthwise along one side of the backbone. With the skin side up, pull the body open, pressing firmly until the bones begin to crack and the bird lays reasonably flat.

Thread sturdy metal skewers through each side of the flattened bird. The skewers should pass perpendicular to the thigh bones into the breasts and out through the middle of the wing joints.

Carving a Turkey

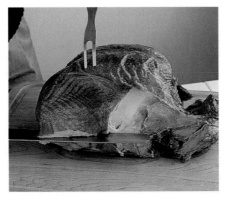

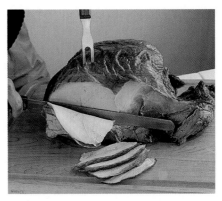

Place the turkey breast side up on a carving board. To remove the legs, cut through the skin and meat between the thighs and breast, exposing the hip joints. Then bend the thighs down and sever them at the joints. Cut the legs between the thighs and the drumsticks severing them at the joints.

To begin carving the breast, first run the blade horizontally into one side of the turkey just above the wing joint, cutting all the way through to the ribs. Repeat on the other side of the turkey.

Next, release slices of breast meat by running the blade vertically down to the horizontal incisions you just made. To free the meat near the bone, follow the contour of the ribs.

Glossary

BASTE
Seasoned liquid brushed over food as it cooks to keep surface moist and add flavor

BUTTERFLY
To make a horizontal cut through middle of a thick piece of meat, leaving about 1 inch (2.5 cm) uncut, and then opening piece out and flattening it

CARVING BOARD
Wooden board with a well for catching juices from meat as it is being carved

CHARCOAL BRIQUETS
Compact 2-inch (5-cm) pieces of fuel made of charcoal and additives; when ignited, they provide even heat for cooking

CHAR-BASKET™ FUEL HOLDERS
Hold charcoal against sides of grill to provide a larger cooking area when Indirect Method is used; charcoal rails serve the same function

COOKING GRATE
Metal grill on which food is cooked; hinged sides facilitate addition of charcoal briquets

DEGLAZE
To loosen drippings on bottom of a roasting or frying pan by stirring in wine, stock, or another liquid

DIRECT METHOD
Grilling technique, used for small or thin cuts of meat and other foods that cook in less than 25 minutes; the food is cooked directly over heat source and turned once halfway through grilling time; on a gas grill, used only for preheating and searing

DRY RUB
Highly concentrated blend of herbs and spices that is rubbed all over food before cooking to impart flavor

DRIP PAN
Foil pan placed beneath food to catch melted fat and juices when food is cooked by Indirect Method

GLAZE
To coat with a baste or sauce, so as to give a sheen to cooked food

GRIDDLE
Heavy, flat pan with a metal handle usually made of cast iron and used to cook breakfast fare, fajitas, or grilled sandwiches

GRILL BRUSH
Stiff brass bristle brush used for removing stubborn food residue from the cooking grate

GRILLING
Cooking food on a metal grate over a heat source (charcoal, gas, or electric coil)

INDIRECT METHOD
Grilling technique, used primarily for larger cuts of meat and other foods that require cooking times longer than 25 minutes; food is cooked by reflected heat (not directly above heat source), sealing in juices and eliminating the need for turning; this method can only be used with a covered grill

INSTANT-READ THERMOMETER
Type of meat thermometer that registers the internal temperature of food within seconds of being inserted; they are not safe for use in the oven

MARINADE
Seasoned liquid (usually containing an acidic ingredient, such as vinegar, wine, or citrus juice) in which food soaks, tenderizing it and enhancing flavor

SEAR
To brown meat directly above heat source at a high temperature, for just a brief time, to seal in juices

SKEWER
Thin metal or bamboo sticks of various lengths on which pieces of meat, poultry, fish, or vegetables are secured prior to grilling

SPATULA
Flat, thin tool used to turn and lift foods on the grill

TONGS
Tool used to grasp and turn foods; usually made of metal with two pieces joined at one end

WOOD CHIPS
Small chips of dried, fragrant hardwoods used to impart a smoky flavor to foods

WOOD CHUNKS
Chunks of dried, fragrant hardwoods used either as a fuel or to add smoky flavor to foods as they cook

ZEST
Thin, outermost layer of peel (colored part only) of citrus fruits

Betty's Grilled Chicken

Chicken on the grill can be a hassle-free weekday meal, particularly if you stick to the basics. You'll love the moist results, whether you're grilling a whole chicken or parts.

Charcoal	Indirect
Gas	Indirect/Medium Heat Searing (optional) see page 6
Grilling time	30–35 minutes

2   large whole chicken breasts, about 1 pound (455 g) *each,* split

¼   teaspoon salt

⅛   teaspoon pepper

Very Easy

Orange-Ginger Chicken Breasts

Basic Chicken Breasts

Remove and discard excess fat from chicken. Rinse and pat dry. Remove skin, if desired. Sprinkle with salt and pepper. Arrange chicken, bone side down, in center of cooking grate. Place lid on grill. Cook until meat near bone is no longer pink (30 to 35 minutes; cut to test).

MAKES 4 SERVINGS.

Per serving: 242 calories (37% from fat), 10 g total fat (3 g saturated fat), 103 g cholesterol, 222 mg sodium, 0 g carbohydrates, 0 g fiber, 37 g protein, 18 mg calcium, 1 mg iron

Charcoal	Indirect
Gas	Indirect/Medium Heat Searing (optional) see page 6
Grilling time	30–35 minutes

⅓   cup (80 ml) orange marmalade

2   tablespoons soy sauce

½   teaspoon ground ginger

1   tablespoon minced onion

     Basic Chicken Breasts (see above)

Orange-Ginger Chicken Breasts

In a 1- to 1½-quart (950-ml to 1.4-liter) pan, stir marmalade, soy sauce, ginger, and onion over medium heat, until hot. Set aside. Follow directions for Basic Chicken Breasts, brushing chicken occasionally with marmalade mixture during last 15 minutes of cooking time.

MAKES 4 SERVINGS.

Per serving: 313 calories (28% from fat), 10 g total fat (3 g saturated fat), 103 mg cholesterol, 616 mg sodium, 19 g carbohydrates, 0 g fiber, 37 g protein, 29 mg calcium, 2 mg iron

Charcoal	Indirect
Gas	Indirect/Medium Heat Searing (optional) see page 6
Grilling time	30–60 minutes

1 chicken, 3 to 3½ pounds
(1.35 to 1.6 kg), halved or
cut up

Salt and pepper

Basic Chicken Halves & Parts

Remove and discard excess fat from chicken. Rinse and pat dry. Remove skin, if desired. Season to taste with salt and pepper.

Arrange chicken, bone side down, in center of cooking grate. Place lid on grill. Cook until meat near bone is no longer pink (30 to 35 minutes for breasts, 35 to 45 minutes for thighs and drumsticks, and 50 to 60 minutes for halves; cut to test).

MAKES 4 SERVINGS.

Per serving: 388 calories (53% from fat), 22 g total fat (6 g saturated fat), 143 mg cholesterol, 133 mg sodium, 0 g carbohydrates, 0 g fiber, 44 g protein, 24 mg calcium, 2 mg iron

Charcoal	Indirect
Gas	Indirect/Medium Heat
Grilling time	1–1½ hours

1 chicken, 3½ to 4 pounds
(1.6 to 1.8 kg)

1 tablespoon olive oil

Salt and pepper

Basic Whole Chicken

Remove neck and giblets from chicken; reserve for other uses. Remove and discard excess fat. Rinse chicken inside and out and pat dry. Brush with oil. Season inside and out with salt and pepper. Secure skin over cavities with small metal skewers. Tie legs together and twist wing tips under back.

Arrange chicken, breast side up, in center of cooking grate. Place lid on grill. Cook until an instant-read thermometer inserted in thickest part of thigh (not touching bone) registers 180°F/82°C (1 to 1½ hours). Transfer chicken to a platter. Let stand for 15 minutes before carving.

MAKES 4 SERVINGS.

Per serving: 463 calories (54% from fat), 27 g total fat (7g saturated fat), 165 g cholesterol, 154 mg sodium, 0 g carbohydrates, 0 g fiber, 51 g protein, 28 mg calcium, 2 mg iron

Lemon-Rosemary Chicken

Rosemary, garlic, and whole lemons—juice plus peel—deliver a big dose of classic Mediterranean taste to this succulent dish.

Charcoal	Indirect
Gas	Indirect/Medium Heat Searing (optional) see page 6
Marinating time	4 hours or until next day
· Grilling time	35–45 minutes

1   chicken, about 3½ pounds (1.6 kg), cut up

3   large lemons

¼   cup (60 ml) olive oil or salad oil

½   cup (120 ml) fresh rosemary or 3 tablespoons dried rosemary

6   cloves garlic, minced or pressed

    Rosemary sprigs

    Lemon wedges

    Salt and pepper

Very Easy

Remove and discard excess fat from chicken. Rinse chicken and pat dry.

Cut lemons in half and ream juice to make ¾ cup (180 ml). Combine reamed lemon shells, lemon juice, oil, the ½ cup (120 ml) rosemary, and garlic in a large heavy-duty plastic food bag or nonreactive bowl. Add chicken and seal bag (or cover bowl). Rotate bag to distribute marinade and place in a shallow pan. Refrigerate for at least 4 hours or until next day, turning chicken occasionally.

Remove chicken from bag, reserving marinade. Arrange chicken, bone side down, in center of cooking grate. Place lid on grill. Cook, brushing occasionally with reserved marinade, until meat near bone is no longer pink (30 to 35 minutes for breasts, 35 to 45 minutes for thighs and drumsticks; cut to test). Transfer chicken to a platter or individual plates. Garnish with rosemary sprigs and lemon wedges. Season to taste with salt and pepper.

MAKES 4 SERVINGS.

Per serving: 493 calories (58% from fat), 31 g total fat (8 g saturated fat), 154 mg cholesterol, 145 mg sodium, 4 g carbohydrates, 0 g fiber, 48 g protein, 48 mg calcium, 3 mg iron

Herb-Mustard Chicken

A quartered chicken goes to the grill clothed in a mustardy herbed marinade. It's an easy family pleaser that's good cold too.

Charcoal	Indirect
Gas	Indirect/Medium Heat Searing (optional) see page 6
Marinating time	4 hours or until next day
Grilling time	35–45 minutes

1   chicken, 3 to 3½ pounds (1.35 to 1.6 kg), cut up

½   cup (120 ml) *each* dry white wine and salad oil

6   tablespoons wine vinegar

2   tablespoons finely chopped onion

1   teaspoon Italian herb seasoning or ¼ teaspoon *each* dried basil, dried marjoram, dried oregano, and dried thyme

2   cloves garlic, minced or pressed

½   teaspoon pepper

¼   cup (60 ml) spicy brown mustard

Salt

Very Easy

Remove and discard excess fat from chicken. Rinse and pat dry.

Combine wine, oil, vinegar, onion, Italian seasoning, garlic, pepper, and mustard in a large heavy-duty plastic food bag. Add chicken and seal bag securely. Rotate bag to distribute marinade and place in a shallow pan. Refrigerate for at least 4 hours or until next day, turning bag occasionally.

Remove chicken from bag and drain, reserving marinade. Arrange chicken, skin side up, in center of cooking grate. Place lid on grill. Cook, brushing occasionally with reserved marinade, until meat near bone is no longer pink (30 to 35 minutes for breasts; 35 to 45 minutes for thighs and drumsticks; cut to test). Season to taste with salt.

MAKES 4 SERVINGS.

Per serving: 652 calories (70% from fat), 50 g total fat (10 g saturated fat), 143 mg cholesterol, 290 mg sodium, 3 g carbohydrates, 0 g fiber, 45 g protein, 32 mg calcium, 2 mg iron

Chicken Legs with Olives

These legs get their Mediterranean flavor from olives, rosemary, and garlic stuffed under the skin. Slices of eggplant join the chicken on the grill; all are brushed with a mixture of honey and orange juice to make a sweet glazed coating.

Charcoal	Indirect
Gas	Indirect/Medium Heat Searing (optional) see page 6
Grilling time	35–45 minutes

4	whole chicken legs with thighs attached, about 2⅔ pounds (1.21 kg) *total*
½	cup (120 ml) green olives, chopped
1	clove garlic, minced or pressed
1	teaspoon minced fresh rosemary or ½ teaspoon crumbled dried rosemary
1	medium-size eggplant, cut crosswise into ¾-inch (2-cm) rounds
2	tablespoons olive oil
2	tablespoons orange juice
2	teaspoons honey

Remove and discard excess fat from chicken. Rinse and pat dry. Cut a slit just through skin at joint on outside of each chicken leg. Slide your fingers between meat and skin to separate it from thigh and drumstick, leaving skin in place. In a small bowl, combine olives, garlic, and rosemary. Tuck olive mixture under skin on top side of each leg, pushing to distribute evenly. (At this point, you may cover and refrigerate until next day.)

Brush both sides of eggplant with oil. In a small bowl, combine orange juice and honey; set aside. Arrange chicken in center of cooking grate. Place lid on grill. Cook for 20 minutes. Add eggplant to grill. Cook, turning eggplant once halfway through cooking time and brushing food with honey mixture, until eggplant is very soft when pressed and meat near thighbone is no longer pink (15 to 25 more minutes; cut to test).

Transfer chicken and eggplant to a platter or individual plates.

Makes 4 servings.

Per serving: 465 calories (57% from fat), 29 g total fat (7 g saturated fat), 138 mg cholesterol, 542 mg sodium, 10 g carbohydrates, 2 g fiber, 40 g protein, 63 mg calcium, 3 mg iron

Whether you're serving mild white-breasted chicken, succulent duck, moist and lean turkey, or gamey pheasant, you'll appreciate how well these easy-to-make side dishes complement your main course.

Papaya with Lime Butter

Charcoal	Direct
Gas	Indirect/Medium Heat
Grilling time	5–8 minutes

2	medium-size firm-ripe papayas, peeled
½	cup (120 ml) butter, melted
2	tablespoons lime juice
½	teaspoon shredded lime zest
	Salt

Cut papayas lengthwise into quarters; discard seeds. In a small bowl, combine butter, lime juice, and lime zest. Lightly brush butter mixture all over papayas. Arrange papayas on cooking grate. Place lid on grill. Cook until fruit is hot and beginning to brown on edges (5 to 8 minutes). Season to taste with salt.

MAKES 8 SERVINGS.

Per serving: 132 calories (76% from fat), 12 g total fat (7 g saturated fat), 31 mg cholesterol, 120 mg sodium, 8 g carbohydrates, 1 g fiber, 1 g protein, 22 mg calcium, 0 mg iron

Very Easy

Roasted Potatoes with Basil

Charcoal	Direct
Gas	Indirect/Medium Heat
Grilling time	30–40 minutes

¼	cup (60 ml) extra-virgin olive oil
16	small red potatoes, about 1½ inches (3.5 cm) in diameter, scrubbed and halved
2	tablespoons *each* lemon juice and grated lemon zest
½	cup (120 ml) finely shredded fresh basil
	Salt and pepper

Lightly brush some of the oil all over potatoes. Arrange potatoes, cut side down, on cooking grate. Place lid on grill. Cook, turning once halfway through cooking time, until potatoes are tender when pierced (30 to 40 minutes).

In a large bowl, combine potatoes, remaining oil, lemon juice, and lemon zest. Let cool. Just before serving, stir in basil. Season to taste with salt and pepper.

MAKES 8 TO 10 SERVINGS.

Per serving: 125 calories (45% from fat), 6 g total fat (1 g saturated fat), 0 mg cholesterol, 8 mg sodium, 16 g carbohydrates, 1 g fiber, 2 g protein, 23 mg calcium, 1 mg iron

Very Easy

Barley, Corn & Onion Salad

Charcoal	Direct
Gas	Indirect/Medium Heat
Grilling time	10–12 minutes

4½	cups (1 liter) chicken broth
1½	cups (360 ml) pearl barley
1	tablespoon grated lemon zest
4	large ears corn, husks and silk removed
2	large red onions, cut in half
2	cups (470 ml) lightly packed fresh mint, minced
½	cup (120 ml) *each* minced cilantro and rice vinegar
½	teaspoon pepper
	Salt

In a 3- to 4-quart (2.8- to 3.8-liter) pan, bring broth, barley, and lemon zest to a boil over high heat; reduce heat, cover, and simmer until barley is tender to bite (about 30 minutes). Drain, reserving broth.

Arrange corn and onions on cooking grate. Place lid on grill. Cook, turning vegetables occasionally, until some kernels are lightly browned and remainder are translucent and onions are golden (10 to 12 minutes). Let cool.

Cut kernels from cobs, discarding cobs; chop onions. In a large bowl, combine corn, onions, barley, mint, cilantro, vinegar, pepper, and enough of the reserved broth to moisten salad. Season to taste with salt.

MAKES 8 TO 10 SERVINGS.

Per serving: 227 calories (9% from fat), 2 g total fat (0 g saturated fat), 0 mg cholesterol, 521 mg sodium, 47 g carbohydrates, 9 g fiber, 8 g protein, 37 mg calcium, 2 mg iron

Lowfat

Stuffed Chicken Legs with Bell Peppers

A fragrant blend of cilantro, basil, and Parmesan pushed gently under the skin of these chicken legs flavors both drumstick and thigh. The whole red peppers that grill alongside provide a colorful accompaniment.

Charcoal	Indirect
Gas	Indirect/Medium Heat Searing (optional) see page 6
Grilling time	35–45 minutes

½   cup (120 ml) *each* firmly packed cilantro, fresh basil, and grated Parmesan cheese

3   whole chicken legs with thighs attached, about 1½ pounds (680 g) *total*

3   large red bell peppers

    Salt and pepper

In a food processor or blender, whirl cilantro, basil, and cheese until minced.

Remove and discard excess fat from chicken. Rinse and pat dry. Cut a slit just through skin at joint on outside of each chicken leg. Slide your fingers between meat and skin to separate it from thigh and drumstick, leaving skin in place. Tuck cilantro mixture under skin on top side of each leg, pushing to distribute evenly.

Arrange chicken in center of cooking grate; lay bell peppers around chicken. Place lid on grill. Cook, turning bell peppers occasionally, until skin chars and blackens (about 20 minutes). Remove peppers from grill and let cool. Continue to cook chicken until meat near thighbone is no longer pink (15 to 25 more minutes; cut to test). Meanwhile, remove skin, stems, and seeds from bell peppers.

Transfer peppers and chicken to a platter. Cut thighs and drumsticks apart. Season to taste with salt and pepper.

Makes 6 servings.

Per serving: 196 calories (45% from fat), 10 g total fat (3 g saturated fat), 57 mg cholesterol, 176 mg sodium, 9 g carbohydrates, 2 g fiber, 19 g protein, 143 mg calcium, 2 mg iron

**GRILL BY THE BOOK
T I P**

To more easily remove the skins from grilled peppers, sweat them in a paper or plastic bag.

Poultry in Romaine Wraps

Romaine lettuce leaves make an agreeable wrapper for prosciutto-wrapped chicken or turkey breast pieces. The lettuce bundles not only are attractive but also help keep the poultry moist.

Charcoal	Direct
Gas	Indirect/Medium Heat
Grilling time	20–25 minutes

Green Dressing (see below)

4   skinless, boneless chicken breast halves, about 1½ pounds (680 g) *total;* or 1 pound (455 g) skinless, boneless turkey breast, cut into 4 logs, *each* 1 to 1½ inches (2.5 to 3.5 cm) thick

4   medium-size romaine lettuce leaves

4   thin slices, about 2 ounces (55 g) *total,* prosciutto

Salt and pepper

Green Dressing

⅓   cup (80 ml) olive oil or salad oil

¼   cup (60 ml) white wine vinegar

2   tablespoons minced onion

1   tablespoon minced parsley

2   teaspoons minced fresh sage or ¾ teaspoon dried sage

2   teaspoons minced fresh thyme or ¾ teaspoon dried thyme

In a blender or food processor, combine ingredients for Green Dressing. Whirl until smooth; set aside.

Rinse poultry and pat dry. In a wide frying pan, bring about 1 inch (2.5 cm) water to a boil over high heat. Add lettuce; cook for 1 minute. Remove, immerse in ice water until cool, and drain; pat dry.

Wrap each poultry piece in 1 prosciutto slice and then in 1 lettuce leaf. Arrange bundles on cooking grate. Place lid on grill. Cook, turning once halfway through cooking time, until meat in thickest part is no longer pink (about 20 minutes for chicken, about 25 minutes for turkey; cut to test).

Cut bundles across grain into slices about 1 inch (2.5 cm) thick. Arrange, cut side up, on individual plates. Serve with dressing. Season to taste with salt and pepper.

MAKES 4 SERVINGS.

Per serving: 387 calories (52% from fat), 22 g total fat (3 g saturated fat), 110 mg cholesterol, 376 mg sodium, 2 g carbohydrates, 1 g fiber, 44 g protein, 38 mg calcium, 2 mg iron

Mike's Ricotta-stuffed Chicken Breasts

These moist, succulent chicken roll-ups are simple to make but fancy enough for company.
Chicken breast halves are pounded thin and spread with
an herbed ricotta-Parmesan mixture; then they're rolled up and sprinkled with more herbs.

Charcoal	Direct
Gas	Indirect/Medium Heat
Grilling time	10–15 minutes

8   ounces (230 g) part-skim ricotta cheese

¼   cup (60 ml) grated Parmesan cheese

1   egg yolk

2   tablespoons minced parsley

1   tablespoon minced fresh basil or 1 teaspoon dried basil

1   tablespoon minced fresh tarragon or 1 teaspoon dried tarragon

1   clove garlic, minced or pressed

8   skinless, boneless chicken breast halves, about 5 ounces (140 g) *each*

2   teaspoons olive oil or salad oil

   Paprika

Lowfat

In a small bowl, combine ricotta, Parmesan, egg yolk, parsley, half the basil, half the tarragon, and garlic.

Rinse chicken and pat dry. With a flat-surfaced mallet, pound each breast between 2 sheets of plastic wrap into a rectangle about ⅛ inch (3 mm) thick. Spread cheese mixture evenly over each breast. Starting with a long side, fold edges in and roll to enclose filling. Fasten rolls with wooden picks.

Brush rolls with oil and sprinkle with paprika and remaining basil and tarragon. Arrange on cooking grate. Place lid on grill. Cook, turning once halfway through cooking time, until meat in center is no longer pink (10 to 15 minutes; cut to test). Remove picks and slice rolls. Arrange slices on individual plates.

MAKES 8 SERVINGS.

Per serving: 229 calories (27% from fat), 7 g total fat (3 g saturated fat), 120 mg cholesterol, 179 mg sodium, 2 g carbohydrates, 0 g fiber, 38 g protein, 145 mg calcium, 1 mg iron

Chicken & Vegetables with Sesame Sauce

Freshly toasted sesame seeds are blended into a smooth ginger-scented sauce to serve with grilled marinated chicken legs, crookneck squash, and shiitake mushrooms.

Charcoal	Indirect
Gas	Indirect/Medium Heat Searing (optional) see page 6
Marinating time	30 minutes–2 hours
Grilling time	35–45 minutes

Sesame Sauce (see below)

½ cup (120 ml) dry sherry or sake

2 tablespoons soy sauce

1 tablespoon Oriental sesame oil or salad oil

4 whole chicken legs with thighs attached, about 2¼ pounds (1.02 kg) *total*

8 green onions, ends trimmed

4 small crookneck squash, cut in half lengthwise

8 large fresh shiitake or regular mushrooms, stems removed

Sesame Sauce

½ cup (120 ml) sesame seeds

3 tablespoons oil

2 tablespoons *each* lemon juice and soy sauce

2 tablespoons minced fresh ginger

1 tablespoon sugar

1 clove garlic

⅛ teaspoon ground red pepper (cayenne)

To prepare Sesame Sauce, toast sesame seeds in a small frying pan over medium heat, shaking pan often, until golden (about 10 minutes). Transfer hot seeds to a blender, add oil, and whirl until a fine paste forms. Add lemon juice, soy sauce, ginger, sugar, garlic, red pepper, and ¼ cup (60 ml) water; whirl until smooth. If made ahead, cover and refrigerate for up to 2 days. If too thick, thin with water before serving.

In a small bowl, combine sherry, soy sauce, and oil. Rinse chicken and pat dry. Place in a large heavy-duty plastic food bag. Place onions, squash, and mushrooms in another bag. Pour half the sherry marinade into each bag and seal securely. Rotate bags to distribute marinade and place in a shallow pan. Refrigerate for at least 30 minutes or up to 2 hours, turning bags occasionally.

Remove chicken and vegetables from bags and drain, reserving marinade. Arrange chicken in center of cooking grate. Place lid on grill. Cook for 15 minutes; add vegetables. Cook, turning vegetables once and brushing food with reserved marinade halfway through cooking time, until vegetables are lightly browned and tender when pierced (5 to 10 minutes for onions, 10 to 15 minutes for mushrooms, and about 20 minutes for squash) and chicken near bone is no longer pink (20 to 30 more minutes; cut to test). Remove food from grill as done and keep warm. Serve with sauce.

MAKES 4 SERVINGS.

Per serving: 759 calories (72% from fat), 58 g total fat (10 g saturated fat), 116 mg cholesterol, 1151 mg sodium, 16 g carbohydrates, 1 g fiber, 36 g protein, 72 mg calcium, 4 mg iron

GRILL BY THE BOOK
T I P

If fresh wild mushrooms are not available, use dry ones. Reconstitute them in warm water, drain, rinse well, and use as needed.

Jamaican Jerk Chicken with Fettuccine

Jerk is a seasoning mixture, probably used originally in Jamaica to preserve wild boar and other meats. The fragrant, spicy paste does double duty here, forming a deeply flavorful coating for grilled chicken breasts and enlivening the creamy pasta sauce.

Charcoal	Direct
Gas	Indirect/Medium Heat
Marinating time	20 minutes or until next day
Grilling time	About 10 minutes

Jerk Seasoning Paste
(see below)

4   skinless, boneless chicken breast halves, about 1 pound (455 g) *total*

2   cups (470 ml) chicken broth

¼   cup (60 ml) whipping cream

12 ounces (340 g) dried fettuccine

Cilantro sprigs

Lime wedges

Salt

Jerk Seasoning Paste

¼   cup (60 ml) firmly packed cilantro

3   tablespoons *each* water and minced fresh ginger

2   tablespoons whole black peppercorns

1   tablespoon *each* ground allspice and brown sugar

2   cloves garlic

½   teaspoon crushed red pepper flakes

¼   teaspoon *each* ground coriander and ground nutmeg

Lowfat

In a blender or food processor, combine ingredients for Jerk Seasoning Paste. Whirl until smooth. Reserve 1 tablespoon of the seasoning; cover and refrigerate. Rinse chicken and pat dry. Coat with remaining seasoning paste. Cover and refrigerate for at least 20 minutes or until next day.

In a wide frying pan, boil reserved seasoning, broth, and cream over high heat, stirring, until reduced to 1½ cups/360 ml (about 10 minutes). Keep warm.

Arrange chicken on cooking grate. Place lid on grill. Cook, turning once halfway through cooking time, until meat in thickest part is no longer pink (about 10 minutes; cut to test). Meanwhile, bring 3 quarts (2.8 liters) water to a boil in a 5- to 6-quart (5- to 6-liter) pan over high heat.

Transfer chicken to a board with a well; keep warm. At once, add fettuccine to boiling water and cook just until tender to bite (about 8 minutes). Drain well; return to pan and add seasoned broth. Mix pasta with 2 forks over medium heat until most of the broth is absorbed; add any juices drained from chicken. Spoon pasta onto individual plates, top with chicken, and garnish with cilantro. Serve with lime wedges. Season to taste with salt.

MAKES 4 SERVINGS.

Per serving: 602 calories (16% from fat), 11 g total fat (4.5 g saturated fat), 196 g cholesterol, 165 mg sodium, 70 g carbohydrates, 2 g fiber, 53 g protein, 75 mg calcium, 6 mg iron

Yakitori Chicken & Vegetables

Chicken, eggplants, and mushrooms all grill together for this satisfying entrée. Start the eggplants cooking first; then add the chicken and mushrooms.

Charcoal	Direct
Gas	Indirect/Medium Heat
Marinating time	1–8 hours
Grilling time	25–27 minutes

2	tablespoons sesame seeds
3	large whole chicken breasts, about 1½ pounds (680 g) *each*, skinned, boned, and split
⅓	cup (80 ml) dry sherry
3	tablespoons *each* soy sauce and Oriental sesame oil
2	teaspoons finely minced fresh ginger
6	medium-size Oriental eggplants
15	to 18 large fresh shiitake or regular mushrooms, stems trimmed flush with caps

In a small frying pan, toast sesame seeds over medium heat, shaking pan often, until golden (about 3 minutes); set aside.

Rinse chicken and pat dry. Cut each breast half into 6 or 7 equal-size cubes and place in a large heavy-duty plastic food bag or nonreactive bowl. In another bowl, combine sherry, soy sauce, oil, and ginger. Pour ¼ cup (60 ml) of the marinade over chicken and seal bag (or cover bowl); reserve remaining marinade. Rotate bag to distribute marinade and place in a shallow pan. Refrigerate for at least 1 hour or up to 8 hours, turning meat occasionally.

Remove chicken from bag and drain, discarding marinade in bag. Thread chicken on 6 skewers; set aside.

Starting about ½ inch (1 cm) from stem end, cut each eggplant lengthwise 3 or 4 times, leaving pieces attached at stem end. Arrange eggplants on cooking grate; gently fan slices out. Place lid on grill. Cook for 15 minutes. Meanwhile, dip mushrooms in reserved marinade. Turn eggplants and add mushrooms and chicken skewers to grill. Continue to cook, turning mushrooms and chicken once halfway through cooking time, until eggplants are very tender when pierced, mushrooms are browned, and meat in center is no longer pink (10 to 12 more minutes; cut chicken to test).

Arrange chicken, mushrooms, and eggplants on a platter or individual plates. Moisten food with reserved marinade and sprinkle with sesame seeds. Serve with any remaining marinade.

MAKES 6 SERVINGS.

Per serving: 215 calories (42% from fat), 10 g total fat (1 g saturated fat), 43 mg cholesterol, 570 mg sodium, 9 g carbohydrates, 2 g fiber, 20 g protein, 64 mg calcium, 2 mg iron

Chicken-on-a-stick with Couscous

Compose a balanced meal with very little effort by serving cubes of marinated chicken breast on skewers, fluffy green onion–studded couscous, and a calcium-rich yogurt sauce flavored with cilantro, garlic, and cumin.

Charcoal	Direct
Gas	Indirect/Medium Heat
Marinating time	15 minutes–4 hours
Grilling time	9–10 minutes

Cumin-Garlic Yogurt Sauce (see below)

⅓	cup (80 ml) lemon juice
⅓	cup (80 ml) olive oil or salad oil
¼	cup (60 ml) dry white wine
6	cloves garlic, minced or pressed
2	bay leaves, crumbled
1¼	pounds (565 g) skinless, boneless chicken breast
2½	cups (590 ml) chicken broth
1	tablespoon butter or margarine
1⅔	cups (400 ml) couscous
½	cup (120 ml) thinly sliced green onions
	Pepper
	Salt

Cumin-Garlic Yogurt Sauce

1½	cups (360 ml) plain yogurt
2	tablespoons minced cilantro
1	clove garlic, minced or pressed
1	teaspoon cumin seeds

Lowfat

In a small bowl, combine ingredients for Cumin-Garlic Yogurt Sauce. Cover and refrigerate for at least 15 minutes or until next day.

Combine lemon juice, oil, wine, garlic, and bay leaves in a large heavy-duty plastic food bag or nonreactive bowl. Rinse chicken and pat dry. Cut into ¾-inch (2-cm) cubes and add to bag. Seal bag (or cover bowl). Rotate bag to distribute marinade and place in a shallow pan. Refrigerate for at least 15 minutes or up to 4 hours, turning chicken occasionally.

In a 2- to 3-quart (1.9- to 2.8-liter) pan, bring broth and butter to a boil over high heat. Stir in couscous. Cover and remove from heat; let stand until liquid is absorbed (about 5 minutes). Stir in onions and season to taste with pepper. Cover and keep warm.

Remove chicken from bag and drain, reserving marinade. Thread chicken on 8 skewers, dividing evenly. Arrange on cooking grate. Place lid on grill. Cook, turning once and brushing with reserved marinade halfway through cooking time, until meat is lightly browned and no longer pink in center (9 to 10 minutes; cut to test).

Stir couscous with a fork and spoon onto a platter or individual plates. Arrange skewers over couscous. Serve with yogurt sauce. Season to taste with salt and pepper.

MAKES 4 SERVINGS.

Per serving: 641 calories (27% from fat), 18 g total fat (5 g saturated fat), 101 mg cholesterol, 799 mg sodium, 66 g carbohydrates, 3 g fiber, 47 g protein, 161 mg calcium, 3 mg iron

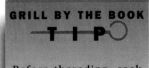

GRILL BY THE BOOK
T·I·P

Before threading, soak bamboo skewers in water to reduce the risk of burning them.

BASTES, RUBS & MARINADES FOR POULTRY

Adaptable poultry takes on a whole new character when it's marinated before cooking or brushed with a seasoned butter or sauce as it sizzles on the grill. Mild and mellow in flavor, poultry takes readily to a wide range of marinades and sauces, from herb-seasoned and tart citrus mixtures to soy-flavored and sweet glazes.

Herb Blend for Poultry

4 teaspoons *each* cracked pepper and dried savory

¼ cup (60 ml) *each* dried basil, rubbed sage, and dried thyme

¼ cup (60 ml) dried lavender (optional)

In a blender, combine pepper, savory, basil, sage, thyme, and, if desired, lavender. Whirl until coarsely ground. Sprinkle herb mixture all over poultry before cooking.

MAKES ABOUT ¾ CUP (180 ML), ENOUGH FOR ABOUT 20 SERVINGS OF POULTRY.

Per serving: 8 calories (15% from fat), 0 g total fat (0 g saturated fat), 0 mg cholesterol, 1 mg sodium, 2 g carbohydrates, 0 g fiber, 0 g protein, 50 mg calcium, 2 mg iron

Salt & Pepper Rub

¼ cup (60 ml) salt

1 tablespoon Szechwan peppercorns

Coarsely grind salt and peppercorns with a rolling pin or a mortar and pestle. Sprinkle salt mixture all over poultry before cooking.

MAKES ABOUT ⅓ CUP (80 ML), ENOUGH FOR 15 TO 20 SERVINGS OF POULTRY.

Per serving: 1 calorie (8% from fat), 0 g total fat (0 g saturated fat), 0 mg cholesterol, 1464 mg sodium, 0 g carbohydrates, 0 g fiber, 0 g protein, 11 mg calcium, 0 mg iron

Bourbon Barbecue Baste

2 tablespoons butter or margarine

2 tablespoons minced onion

2 cloves garlic, minced or pressed

1 can, about 6 ounces (170 g), tomato paste

½ cup (120 ml) *each* bourbon whiskey and water

¼ cup (60 ml) firmly packed brown sugar

2 tablespoons Worcestershire

¼ teaspoon *each* dried basil, dried sage, and dried oregano

6 to 8 drops liquid hot pepper seasoning

In a 3- to 4-quart (2.8- to 3.8-liter) pan, melt butter over medium heat. Add onion and garlic and cook, stirring, until onion is soft (about 10 minutes). Stir in tomato paste, bourbon, water, sugar, Worcestershire, basil, sage, oregano, and hot pepper seasoning to taste. Reduce heat, cover, and simmer until flavors are blended (10 to 15 minutes). Brush basting mixture all over poultry while it cooks.

MAKES ABOUT 1½ CUPS (360 ML), ENOUGH FOR 10 TO 12 SERVINGS OF POULTRY.

Per serving: 80 calories (35% from fat), 2 g total fat (1 g saturated fat), 6 mg cholesterol, 177 mg sodium, 9 g carbohydrates, 1 g fiber, 1 g protein, 13 mg calcium, 1 mg iron

Apricot-Dijon Glaze

¼ cup (60 ml) apricot jam

2 tablespoons *each* chopped dried apricots and Dijon mustard

1 tablespoon chopped shallot

1 teaspoon lemon juice

In a small bowl, combine jam, apricots, mustard, shallot, and lemon juice. Brush poultry occasionally with apricot mixture during last 20 minutes of cooking time.

MAKES ABOUT ½ CUP (120 ML), ENOUGH FOR 3 OR 4 SERVINGS OF POULTRY.

Per serving: 68 calories (1% from fat), 0 g total fat (0 g saturated fat), 0 mg cholesterol, 189 mg sodium, 16 g carbohydrates, 1 g fiber, 0 g protein, 7 mg calcium, 0 mg iron

Ginger-Soy Marinade & Baste

⅔ cup (160 ml) *each* seasoned rice vinegar and mirin (sweetened rice wine)

⅔ cup (160 ml) *each* minced fresh ginger and cilantro

½ cup (120 ml) soy sauce

4 cloves garlic, minced or pressed

In a large bowl, combine vinegar, mirin, ginger, cilantro, soy sauce, and garlic. Marinate poultry in vinegar mixture for at least 1 hour or until next day. Or, to use as a baste, brush mixture all over poultry while it cooks.

MAKES ABOUT 3 CUPS (710 ML), ENOUGH FOR 3 OR 4 SERVINGS OF POULTRY.

Per serving: 173 calories (1% from fat), 0 g total fat (0 g saturated fat), 0 mg cholesterol, 2857 mg sodium, 29 g carbohydrates, 0 g fiber, 3 g protein, 21 mg calcium, 1 mg iron

Sherry Marinade

1½ cups (360 ml) dry sherry

½ cup (1260 ml) soy sauce

¼ cup (60 ml) minced fresh ginger

4 cloves garlic, minced or pressed

1 tablespoon sugar

In a large bowl, combine sherry, soy sauce, ginger, garlic, and sugar. Marinate poultry in sherry mixture for at least 1 hour or until next day.

MAKES ABOUT 2½ CUPS (590 ML), ENOUGH FOR 3 OR 4 SERVINGS OF POULTRY.

Per serving: 153 calories (1% from fat), 0 g total fat (0 g saturated fat), 0 mg cholesterol, 2067 mg sodium, 12 g carbohydrates, 0 g fiber, 2 g protein, 20 mg calcium, 1 mg iron

Sweet Chili Marinade & Baste

1 cup (240 ml) cider vinegar

⅔ cup (160 ml) light or dark molasses

⅔ cup (160 ml) Dijon mustard

¼ cup (60 ml) *each* tomato paste and soy sauce

6 to 8 teaspoons liquid hot pepper seasoning

In a large bowl, combine vinegar, molasses, mustard, tomato paste, soy sauce, and liquid hot pepper seasoning to taste. Marinate poultry in molasses mixture for at least 1 hour or until next day. Or, to use as a baste, brush mixture all over poultry while it cooks.

MAKES ABOUT 2½ CUPS (590 ML), ENOUGH FOR 3 OR 4 SERVINGS OF POULTRY.

Per serving: 220 calories (1% from fat), 0 g total fat (0 g saturated fat), 0 mg cholesterol, 2374 mg sodium, 46 g carbohydrates, 1 g fiber, 2 g protein, 125 mg calcium, 4 mg iron

Chili-Lemon Glaze

¼ cup (60 ml) lemon juice

2 tablespoons honey

1 tablespoon chili powder

¼ teaspoon *each* ground cinnamon and ground red pepper (cayenne)

½ teaspoon salt (optional)

In a small bowl, combine lemon juice, honey, chili powder, cinnamon, and red pepper. Stir in salt, if desired. Brush poultry occasionally with chili mixture during last 20 minutes of cooking time.

MAKES ABOUT ⅓ CUP (80 ML), ENOUGH FOR 3 OR 4 SERVINGS OF POULTRY.

Per serving: 42 calories (7% from fat), 0 g total fat (0 g saturated fat), 0 mg cholesterol, 23 mg sodium, 11 g carbohydrates, 1 g fiber, 0 g protein, 9 mg calcium, 0 mg iron

Chicken Kebabs Shanghai

Sesame oil adds a mellow note to the bright flavors of ground coriander, orange, and ginger, transforming simple kebabs of chicken and fresh pineapple into splendid skewers.

Charcoal	Direct
Gas	Indirect/Medium Heat
Marinating time	30 minutes–8 hours
Grilling time	10–12 minutes

¾   teaspoon grated orange zest

⅓   cup (80 ml) orange juice

3   tablespoons firmly packed brown sugar

2   tablespoons soy sauce

4   teaspoons *each* minced fresh ginger and wine vinegar

1   tablespoon Oriental sesame oil or salad oil

½   teaspoon ground coriander

6   skinless, boneless chicken breast halves, about 1½ pounds (680 g) *total*

1   medium-size red bell pepper, seeded and cut into 1-inch (2.5-cm) squares

12   ounces (340 g) peeled and cored pineapple, cut into 1-inch (2.5-cm) cubes

Combine orange zest, orange juice, sugar, soy sauce, ginger, vinegar, oil, and coriander in a large heavy-duty plastic food bag or nonreactive bowl. Rinse chicken and pat dry. Cut into 1½-inch (3.5-cm) cubes and add to container. Seal bag (or cover bowl). Rotate bag to distribute marinade and place in a shallow pan. Refrigerate for at least 30 minutes or up to 8 hours, turning chicken occasionally.

Remove chicken from bag and drain, reserving marinade. Thread chicken, bell pepper, and pineapple on skewers, alternating pieces. Brush reserved marinade over bell pepper and pineapple. Arrange skewers on cooking grate. Place lid on grill. Cook, turning once halfway through cooking time, until meat in center is no longer pink (10 to 12 minutes; cut to test).

MAKES 6 SERVINGS.

Per serving: 213 calories (17% from fat), 4 g total fat (1 g saturated fat), 66 g cholesterol, 421 mg sodium, 16 g carbohydrates, 1 g fiber, 27 g protein, 27 mg calcium, 1 mg iron

Italian-style Chicken

This no-fuss whole grilled bird gets its great flavor from Italian herb seasoning—a handy mixture that usually includes oregano, rosemary, savory, thyme, marjoram, sage, and basil.

Charcoal	Indirect
Gas	Indirect/Medium Heat
Grilling time	1–1½ hours

1   chicken, 3½ to 4 pounds (1.6 to 1.8 kg)

     Salt and pepper

2   tablespoons olive oil

3   tablespoons lemon juice

1½   teaspoons Italian herb seasoning or ¼ teaspoon *each* dried basil, dried marjoram, dried oregano, and dried thyme

Very Easy

Remove neck and giblets from chicken; reserve for other uses. Remove and discard excess fat. Rinse chicken inside and out and pat dry. Season inside and out with salt and pepper. Secure skin over cavities with small metal skewers. Tie legs together and twist wing tips under back.

In a small bowl, combine oil, lemon juice, and Italian seasoning. Brush mixture over chicken. Arrange chicken, breast side up, in center of cooking grate. Place lid on grill. Cook, brushing occasionally with remaining herb mixture, until an instant-read thermometer inserted in thickest part of thigh (not touching bone) registers 180°F/82°C (1 to 1½ hours). Transfer chicken to a platter. Let stand for 10 minutes before carving.

Makes 4 servings.

Per serving: 480 calories (56% from fat), 29 g total fat (8 g saturated fat), 165 mg cholesterol, 158 mg sodium, 1 g carbohydrates, 0 g fiber, 51 g protein, 29 mg calcium, 2 mg iron

Thai Chicken with Red Chile Sauce

The chicken is split and skewered to make it easy to flip on the grill; butterflying the bird also exposes more meat to be rubbed with the lively Thai seasoning mixture. A sweet-sour chile sauce accompanies the chicken.

Charcoal	Indirect
Gas	Indirect/Medium Heat Searing (optional) see page 6
Marinating time	10 minutes or until next day
Grilling time	50–60 minutes

Red Chile Sauce (see below)

1   chicken, 3 to 3½ pounds (1.35 to 1.6 kg)

6   large cloves garlic, chopped

¼   cup (60 ml) thinly sliced green onions

1   tablespoon chopped fresh ginger

½   teaspoon *each* ground coriander and coarsely ground pepper

2   tablespoons fish sauce (*nam pla* or *nuoc mam*) or soy sauce

Red Chile Sauce

3   large dried California or New Mexico chiles

1   or 2 small dried hot red chiles

¾   cup (180 ml) hot water

3   cloves garlic

½   cup (120 ml) distilled white vinegar

⅓   cup (70 g) sugar

Salt

To prepare Red Chile Sauce, remove stems and seeds from California-and small dried hot red chiles. Rinse, coarsely chop, and place in a bowl. Add water. Soak until soft (about 10 minutes). Transfer to a blender, add garlic, and whirl until coarsely puréed. Place in a 1- to 1½-quart (950-ml to 1.4-liter) pan with vinegar and sugar. Boil over high heat, stirring, until reduced to about ¾ cup/180 ml (about 10 minutes). Season to taste with salt. If made ahead, cover and refrigerate for up to 1 week.

Remove neck and giblets from chicken; reserve for other uses. Remove and discard excess fat. Rinse chicken inside and out and pat dry. With poultry shears or a knife, split chicken lengthwise through breastbone. Place, skin side up, on a flat surface, pull open, and press firmly, cracking bones slightly, until bird lies reasonably flat.

Thread chicken on sturdy metal skewers about 18 inches (46 cm) long, forcing 1 skewer through thigh (perpendicular to bone) into breast and out through middle joint of wing. Repeat on other side of chicken.

With a mortar and pestle or in a blender, grind garlic, onions, ginger, coriander, pepper, and fish sauce into a coarse paste. Pat all over chicken. Cover and refrigerate for at least 10 minutes or until next day.

Arrange chicken in center of cooking grate. Place lid on grill. Cook until meat near thighbone is no longer pink (50 to 60 minutes; cut to test). Remove chicken from skewers. Cut up chicken and serve with chile sauce.

MAKES 4 SERVINGS.

Per serving: 510 calories (42% from fat), 24 g total fat (7 g saturated fat), 143 mg cholesterol, 436 mg sodium, 26 g carbohydrates, 0 g fiber, 47 g protein, 55 mg calcium, 3 mg iron

GRILL BY THE BOOK
T I P

To loosen garlic skin, lightly smash individual cloves of garlic with the flat side of a large knife blade.

Cilantro & Sake Roast Chicken

*A mixture of chopped celery leaves, cilantro, and rosemary
is moistened with sake (Chinese rice wine) and stuffed into the cavity of a whole chicken so that
the meat is suffused with fragrance as it roasts.*

Charcoal	Indirect
Gas	Indirect/Medium Heat
Marinating time	1 hour
Grilling time	1–1½ hours

1   chicken, 3½ to 4 pounds
    (1.6 to 1.8 kg)

    Salt and pepper

1   cup (240 ml) *each* chopped
    celery leaves and chopped
    cilantro

8   fresh rosemary sprigs, *each*
    about 2 inches (5 cm) long, or
    ¾ teaspoon dried rosemary

½   cup (120 ml) sake

Very Easy

Remove neck and giblets from chicken; reserve for other uses. Remove and discard excess fat. Rinse chicken inside and out and pat dry. Season body cavity with salt and pepper.

In a small bowl, combine celery leaves, cilantro, rosemary, and ¼ cup (60 ml) of the sake. Stuff mixture into body cavity of chicken; secure skin over cavities with small metal skewers. Tie legs together and twist wing tips under back. Cover and refrigerate for 1 hour.

Arrange chicken, breast side up, in center of cooking grate. Place lid on grill. Cook, brushing occasionally with remaining sake, until an instant-read thermometer inserted in thickest part of thigh (not touching bone) registers 180°F/82°C (1 to 1½ hours). Remove chicken from grill and discard stuffing. Transfer bird to a platter. Let stand for 10 minutes before carving.

MAKES 4 OR 5 SERVINGS.

Per serving: 451 calories (53% from fat), 26 g total fat (7 g saturated fat), 165 mg cholesterol, 158 mg sodium, 1 g carbohydrates, 0 g fiber, 51 g protein, 41 mg calcium, 3 mg iron

Turkey Kebabs with Onion Banners

A simple-to-make glaze of orange marmalade and mustard gives a robust punch of flavor to these handsome kebabs. Each green onion is threaded onto the skewer so it forms a wavy "banner."

Charcoal	Direct
Gas	Indirect/Medium Heat
Grilling time	About 15 minutes

⅓ cup (80 ml) orange marmalade

2 tablespoons Dijon mustard

1 pound (455 g) skinless, boneless turkey breast or turkey thigh

About 12 green onions

Lemon wedges

Salt

Very Easy

In a small bowl, combine marmalade and mustard; set aside.

Rinse turkey and pat dry. Cut meat into about 1½-inch (3.5-cm) cubes. Trim onion ends so onions are about 6 inches (15 cm) long. Alternately thread meat and onions (through white part only) onto 4 skewers, beginning and ending with meat.

Arrange skewers on cooking grate and brush with some of the marmalade mixture. Place lid on grill. Cook, turning once and brushing with remaining marmalade mixture halfway through cooking time, until meat in center is no longer pink (about 15 minutes for breasts, 18 to 22 minutes for thighs; cut to test). Transfer skewers to a platter or individual plates. Serve with lemon wedges. Season to taste with salt.

Makes 4 servings.

Per serving: 217 calories (3% from fat), 1 g total fat (0 g saturated fat), 80 mg cholesterol, 252 mg sodium, 21 g carbohydrates, 1 g fiber, 30 g protein, 54 mg calcium, 2 mg iron

Turkey Rolls with Shiitake-Cheese Filling

*Pounded turkey breasts are wrapped around a savory mixture
of shiitake mushrooms, two types of cheese, and sun-dried tomatoes. The neat bundles are a
snap to grill and make a lovely presentation for friends or family.*

Charcoal	Direct
Gas	Indirect/Medium Heat
Grilling time	10–12 minutes

8	ounces (230 g) fresh shiitake or regular mushrooms
5	teaspoons oil drained from sun-dried tomatoes packed in olive oil
2	tablespoons minced, drained sun-dried tomatoes
1	clove garlic, minced or pressed
8	skinless, boneless turkey breast slices or cutlets, 2 to 3 ounces (55 to 85 g) *each,* cut about ⅜ inch (9 mm) thick
8	ounces (230 g) fontina cheese, cut into sticks about ¼ inch (6 mm) thick
16	large sage leaves or 1½ teaspoons dried sage
1½	tablespoons minced fresh thyme or 1½ teaspoons dried thyme
½	cup (120 ml) grated Asiago cheese

Cut 4 of the mushrooms in half; coarsely chop remaining mushrooms. Heat 2 teaspoons of the oil in an 8- to 10-inch (20- to 25-cm) frying pan over medium-high heat. Add mushroom halves and cook, stirring, until lightly browned (6 to 8 minutes). Remove from pan and set aside. Heat remaining oil in pan. Add chopped mushrooms, tomatoes, and garlic. Cook, stirring often, until mushrooms begin to brown (6 to 8 minutes); let cool.

With a flat-surfaced mallet, pound each turkey slice between 2 sheets of plastic wrap until about ⅛ inch (3 mm) thick. Lay an eighth of the fontina cheese in center of each turkey slice; top equally with mushroom mixture, sage, thyme, and Asiago. Roll to enclose.

Arrange turkey rolls on cooking grate. Place lid on grill. Cook, turning once halfway through cooking time, until meat in center is no longer pink (10 to 12 minutes; cut to test). Transfer to a platter or individual plates. Garnish with reserved mushroom halves.

MAKES 6 TO 8 SERVINGS.

Per serving: 312 calories (54% from fat), 18 g total fat (9 g saturated fat), 94 mg cholesterol, 395 mg sodium, 3 g carbohydrates, 1 g fiber, 31 g protein, 268 mg calcium, 2 mg iron

Turkey Tenderloins

Perfect for those days when time is short, tender turkey breast tenderloins cook quickly on the grill. The raspberry glaze locks in moisture during broiling and doubles as a sauce.

Charcoal	Direct
Gas	Indirect/Medium Heat
Grilling time	10–12 minutes

½ cup (120 ml) seedless raspberry jam

6 tablespoons raspberry vinegar

¼ cup (60 ml) Dijon mustard

1 teaspoon grated orange zest

½ teaspoon fresh or dried thyme

4 skinless, boneless turkey breast tenderloins, about 1½ pounds (680 g) *total*

Salt

Very Easy

In a 1- to 1½-quart (950-ml to 1.4-liter) pan, whisk jam, vinegar, mustard, orange zest, and thyme. Boil over high heat, stirring, until reduced by about a fourth and slightly thickened (2 to 3 minutes). Set aside ½ cup (120 ml) of the glaze.

Rinse turkey and pat dry. Brush with some of the remaining glaze. Arrange meat on cooking grate. Place lid on grill. Cook, turning once and brushing with remaining glaze halfway through cooking time, until meat in thickest part is no longer pink (10 to 12 minutes; cut to test). Serve with reserved glaze. Season to taste with salt.

MAKES 4 SERVINGS.

Per serving: 305 calories (4% from fat), 1 g total fat (0 g saturated fat), 106 mg cholesterol, 460 mg sodium, 27 g carbohydrates, 0 g fiber, 42 g protein, 29 mg calcium, 2 mg iron

Turkey with Two-tone Tomato Salad

When tomatoes hang heavy on the vine, serve this great summertime main-course salad. Slices of red tomatoes are topped with grilled turkey breast,
a toss of yellow cherry tomatoes with threads of arugula, and a scattering of Parmesan cheese.

Charcoal	Direct
Gas	Indirect/Medium Heat
Grilling time	3–5 minutes

¼ cup (60 ml) balsamic or red wine vinegar

2 tablespoons *each* salad oil and Dijon mustard

3 cups (710 ml) yellow cherry tomatoes

2 cups (470 ml) lightly packed arugula or fresh basil

4 skinless, boneless turkey breast slices, about 12 ounces (340 g) *total*, cut about ¼ inch (6 mm) thick

3 large tomatoes

3 tablespoons shredded Parmesan cheese

Salt

Very Easy

In a large bowl, combine vinegar, oil, and mustard; set aside 3 tablespoons of the dressing. Cut cherry tomatoes in half and mix with dressing in bowl. Cut arugula into fine slivers. Set tomatoes and arugula aside.

Rinse turkey and pat dry. Brush with some of the reserved dressing. Arrange turkey on cooking grate. Place lid on grill. Cook, turning once and brushing with reserved dressing halfway through cooking time, until meat in center is no longer pink (3 to 5 minutes; cut to test).

Slice large tomatoes and arrange on individual plates. Top with turkey. Mix cherry tomatoes and arugula and spoon over turkey. Sprinkle with cheese. Season to taste with salt.

MAKES 4 SERVINGS.

Per serving: 227 calories (37% from fat), 9 g total fat (2 g saturated fat), 63 mg cholesterol, 319 mg sodium, 10 g carbohydrates, 3 g fiber, 26 g protein, 110 mg calcium, 2 mg iron

GRILL BY THE BOOK
T I P

To simplify chopping fresh herbs, stack the leaves; then cut them all at once.

Turkey Cutlets Piccata

*The marinade for these easy and elegant turkey breast cutlets
gets a flavor boost from the piquant liquid in the caper jar. Lemon wedges and a scattering of
capers provide the finishing touches.*

Charcoal	Direct
Gas	Indirect/Medium Heat
Marinating time	30 minutes–2 hours
Grilling time	3–5 minutes

1	pound (455 g) skinless, boneless turkey breast cutlets or slices, cut about ¼ inch (6 mm) thick
1½	tablespoons capers with liquid
¼	cup (60 ml) lemon juice
1	tablespoon olive oil
⅛	teaspoon pepper
	Lemon wedges
	Salt

Very Easy

Rinse turkey and pat dry. Drain caper liquid into a large heavy-duty plastic food bag or nonreactive bowl; set capers aside. Add lemon juice, oil, and pepper. Add turkey and seal bag (or cover bowl). Rotate bag to distribute marinade and place in a shallow pan. Refrigerate for at least 30 minutes or up to 2 hours, turning meat once.

Remove turkey from bag and drain, reserving marinade. Arrange turkey on cooking grate. Place lid on grill. Cook, turning once and brushing with reserved marinade halfway through cooking time, until meat in center is no longer pink (3 to 5 minutes; cut to test). Transfer to a platter or individual plates and sprinkle with capers. Garnish with lemon wedges. Season to taste with salt.

MAKES 2 OR 3 SERVINGS.

Per serving: 212 calories (24% from fat), 6 g total fat (1 g saturated fat), 94 mg cholesterol, 188 mg sodium, 1 g carbohydrates, 0 g fiber, 37 g protein, 18 mg calcium, 2 mg iron

Turkey & Squash with Cranberry Salsa

Squash and cranberries aren't for Thanksgiving only. Here, cranberry salsa and skewers of grilled squash give these traditional turkey accompaniments a new vitality.

Charcoal	Indirect
Gas	Indirect/Medium Heat
Grilling time	About 1 hour 10 minutes

Cranberry Salsa (see below)

1½ pounds (680 g) seeded banana squash, cut into pieces about 1½ by 4 inches (3.5 by 10 cm)

1 pound (455 g) skinless, boneless turkey breast slices or cutlets, cut about ³⁄₈ inch (9 mm) thick

3 turkey drumsticks, about 1½ pounds (680 g) *each*

6 tablespoons olive oil

2 cloves garlic, minced or pressed

Cranberry Salsa

1½ cups (360 ml) fresh or frozen cranberries

½ small onion

¼ cup (60 ml) firmly packed parsley

¼ to ½ teaspoon crushed red pepper flakes

1 teaspoon *each* grated orange zest and lemon juice

2 tablespoons orange juice

1½ tablespoons honey

To prepare Cranberry Salsa, finely chop cranberries, onion, parsley, and red pepper flakes to taste in a food processor or with a large knife. Stir in orange zest, lemon juice, orange juice, and honey. If made ahead, cover and refrigerate for up to 2 days.

Thread 4 or 5 pieces of squash, perpendicular to wide sides, onto a skewer 10 to 12 inches (25 to 30 cm) long. Add another skewer parallel to first and about 1½ inches (3.5 cm) from it. Repeat for remaining squash. Set aside.

Rinse turkey breast and drumsticks and pat dry. In a small bowl, combine oil and garlic. Arrange drumsticks in center of cooking grate. Place lid on grill. Cook for 20 minutes, brushing once with garlic oil. Brush squash with garlic oil and add to grill. Cook, brushing food once with garlic oil halfway through cooking time, until squash is tender when pierced (about 30 minutes) and meat near bone is no longer pink (30 to 40 more minutes; cut to test). Remove from grill and keep warm.

Brush turkey breast slices with garlic oil and arrange on cooking grate. Place lid on grill. Cook, turning once halfway through cooking time, until meat in center is no longer pink (6 to 8 minutes; cut to test). Transfer turkey to a platter. Remove squash from skewers and place alongside. Serve with salsa.

MAKES 8 SERVINGS.

Per serving: 497 calories (45% from fat), 25 g total fat (6 g saturated fat), 150 mg cholesterol, 138 mg sodium, 15 g carbohydrates, 3 g fiber, 53 g protein, 86 mg calcium, 5 mg iron

Grilled Turkey

Grilled turkey is good anytime, but it makes especially good sense during times of the year when you don't want to heat up the house by turning on the oven.
Use the chart on the facing page to guide you on cooking times.

Charcoal	Indirect
Gas	Indirect/Medium Heat
Grilling time	1½ –2 hours

1   bone-in turkey breast half, 3 to 3½ pounds (1.35 to 1.6 kg)

2   teaspoons olive oil or salad oil

    Salt and pepper

Very Easy

Turkey with Chile-Orange Glaze

Basic Turkey Breast

Rinse turkey inside and out and pat dry. Brush with oil. Season to taste with salt and pepper. Arrange turkey, bone side down, in center of cooking grate. Place lid on grill. Cook until an instant-read thermometer inserted in thickest part of breast (not touching bone) registers 170°F/77°C (1 to 1½ hours).

MAKES 5 OR 6 SERVINGS PLUS LEFTOVERS.

Per serving: 219 calories (38% from fat), 9 g total fat (2 g saturated fat), 84 mg cholesterol, 71 mg sodium, 0 g carbohydrates, 0 g fiber, 33 g protein, 24 mg calcium, 2 mg iron

Charcoal	Indirect
Gas	Indirect/Medium Heat
Grilling time	See chart

1 turkey, 10 to 12 pounds
(4.5 to 5.5 kg)

Salt and pepper

1 tablespoon olive oil or
salad oil

Very Easy

Basic Whole Turkey

Discard leg truss from turkey. Remove neck and giblets; reserve for other uses. Remove and discard excess fat. Rinse bird inside and out and pat dry. Season body cavity with salt and pepper. Secure skin over cavities with small metal skewers. Tie legs together and twist wing tips under back. Brush turkey with oil and lightly sprinkle with salt and pepper.

Arrange turkey, breast side up, in center of cooking grate. Place lid on grill. Cook until an instant-read thermometer inserted in thickest part of thigh (not touching bone) registers 180°F/82°C (1½ to 2¼ hours).

Transfer turkey to a platter. Let stand for 15 minutes before carving.

MAKES 10 TO 12 SERVINGS PLUS LEFTOVERS.

Per ¼ pound (115 g) boneless cooked turkey, based on percentages of white and dark meat found in average turkey (including skin): 231 calories (42% from fat), 10 g total fat (3 g saturated fat), 93 mg cholesterol, 82 mg sodium, 0 g carbohydrates, 0 g fiber, 32 g protein, 31 mg calcium, 2 mg iron

Charcoal	Indirect
Gas	Indirect/Medium Heat
Grilling time	See chart

3 tablespoons ground dried
New Mexico or California
chiles; or 3 tablespoons chili
powder

1 large container, 12 ounces
(340 g), frozen orange juice
concentrate, thawed

2 tablespoons grated orange
zest

1 teaspoon ground cumin

1 turkey

Good for a Crowd

Turkey with Chile-Orange Glaze

In a small bowl, combine chiles, orange juice concentrate, orange zest, and cumin; set aside.

Discard leg truss from turkey. Remove turkey neck and giblets; reserve for other uses. Remove and discard excess fat. Rinse bird inside and out and pat dry. Secure skin over cavities with small metal skewers. Tie legs together and twist wing tips under back.

Arrange turkey, breast side up, in center of cooking grate. Place lid on grill. Cook until an instant-read thermometer inserted in thickest part of thigh (not touching bone) registers 180°F (82°C); start checking doneness at least 30 minutes before minimum cooking time shown in chart. About 20 minutes before turkey is done, brush turkey generously with chile glaze. If parts of turkey darken excessively before bird is done, loosely cover those areas with foil. Transfer turkey to a platter. Let stand for 15 minutes before carving.

Per ¼ pound (115 g) boneless cooked turkey, based on percentages of white and dark meat found in average turkey (including skin): 249 calories (39% from fat), 10 g total fat (3 g saturated fat), 93 mg cholesterol, 82 mg sodium, 5 g carbohydrates, 0 g fiber, 32 g protein, 36 mg calcium, 2 mg iron

Cooking Chart for Whole Turkey

Turkey weights (with giblets)	Internal temperature	Cooking time
10 to 13 pounds (4.5 to 5.9 kg)	*180°F (82°C)*	*1½ to 2¼ hours*
14 to 23 pounds (6.4 to 10.4 kg)	*180°F (82°C)*	*2½ to 3½ hours*

Each pound of uncooked turkey will yield one 4-ounce serving (115 g) plus leftovers

Turkey with Tomato Glaze

A tomato glaze works magic on this grill-roasted turkey, coating the bird with the mingled flavors of red wine, dried tomatoes, lime, garlic, and rosemary. The glaze is applied near the end of the cooking time to prevent scorching.

Charcoal	Indirect
Gas	Indirect/Medium Heat
Grilling time	2½–3 hours

1   turkey, 14 to 16 pounds (6.4 to 7.3 kg)

2   ounces (55 g) sun-dried tomatoes (not packed in oil)

⅓   cup (80 ml) *each* dry red wine and chicken broth

3   tablespoons lime juice

2   cloves garlic, minced or pressed

2   teaspoons minced fresh rosemary or 1 teaspoon crumbled dried rosemary

Good for a Crowd

Discard leg truss from turkey. Remove turkey neck and giblets; reserve for other uses. Remove and discard excess fat. Rinse bird inside and out and pat dry. Tie legs together and twist wing tips under back.

Place turkey, breast side up, in center of cooking grate. Place lid on grill. While turkey is cooking, bring tomatoes, wine, broth, lime juice, garlic, and rosemary to a boil in a 3- to 4-quart (2.8- to 3.8-liter) pan over high heat; reduce heat, cover, and simmer until tomatoes are easy to mash (20 to 25 minutes). Transfer mixture to a blender or food processor and whirl until smooth; set aside.

Cook turkey until an instant-read thermometer inserted in thickest part of thigh (not touching bone) registers 180°F/82°C (2½ to 3 hours; start checking for doneness after 2 hours). About 20 minutes before turkey is done, begin brushing occasionally with tomato mixture, using all. If parts of turkey darken excessively before bird is done, loosely cover those areas with foil.

Transfer turkey to a platter. Let stand for 15 minutes before carving.

MAKES 14 TO 16 SERVINGS PLUS LEFTOVERS.

Per ¼ pound (115g) boneless cooked turkey, based on percentages of white and dark meat found in average turkey (including skin): 237 calories (41% from fat), 10 g total fat (3 g saturated fat), 94 mg cholesterol, 95 mg sodium, 1 g carbohydrates, 0 g fiber, 32 g protein, 34 mg calcium, 2 mg iron

GRILL BY THE BOOK
T I P

You can cook stuffing in a foil pan on top of the cooking grate while the bird is grilling.

Orange-Ginger Smoked Turkey

Hickory chips and two whole heads of garlic supply pungent smoke throughout the cooking of this turkey. A glaze made from orange juice and fresh ginger complements the smoky flavor.

Charcoal	Indirect
Gas	Indirect/Medium Heat
Grilling time	2–2½ hours

1   turkey, 12 to 14 pounds (5.5 to 6.4 kg)

1   large onion, quartered

About 4 cups (950 ml) hickory chips

2   medium-size heads garlic, unpeeled, separated into cloves

1   small can, 6 ounces (170 g), frozen orange juice concentrate, thawed

½   cup (120 ml) minced fresh ginger

1   tablespoon salad oil

Good for a Crowd

Discard leg truss from turkey. Remove neck and giblets. Remove and discard excess fat. Rinse bird inside and out; pat dry. Place 2 onion quarters in neck and 2 in body. Secure skin over cavities with small metal skewers. Tie legs together and twist wing tips under back. Soak hickory chips for 30 minutes in enough warm water to make them float. Cut garlic cloves in half and set aside. In a small bowl, combine orange juice concentrate, ginger, and oil.

In a charcoal barbecue, scatter a handful of wood chips and half the garlic onto mounds of coals. *In a gas barbecue,* place chips and half the garlic in a foil pan and set under cooking grate on top of heat source in left front corner of barbecue; turn heat to High and preheat for 10 to 15 minutes. Then turn heat to Indirect/Medium.

Arrange turkey, breast side up, in center of cooking grate. Place lid on grill. Cook, adding more wood chips and garlic every 30 to 35 until an instant-read thermometer inserted in thickest part of thigh (not touching bone) registers 180°F/82°C (2 to 2½ hours; start checking for doneness after 1½ hours). About 45 minutes before turkey is done, begin brushing occasionally with orange juice mixture, using all. If parts of turkey darken excessively before bird is done, loosely cover those areas with foil.

Transfer turkey to a platter. Let stand for 15 minutes before carving.

MAKES 12 TO 14 SERVINGS PLUS LEFTOVERS.

Per ¼ pound (115 g) boneless cooked turkey, based on percentages of white and dark meat found in average turkey (including skin): 271 calories (40% from fat), 11 g total fat (3 g saturated fat), 113 mg cholesterol, 155 mg sodium, 5 g carbohydrates, 0 g fiber, 34 g protein, 36 mg calcium, 3 mg iron

Jerry's Rosemary-smoked Turkey

When a flourishing garden or a friendly neighbor provides you with an abundance of fresh rosemary, try this grilled turkey. Sprigs of the fragrant herb are pushed through the cooking grate to create an aromatic smoke.

Charcoal	Indirect
Gas	Indirect/Medium Heat
Grilling time	2½–3 hours

12	ounces (340 g) fresh rosemary sprigs
3	tablespoons olive oil or salad oil
2	tablespoons minced fresh rosemary
1	tablespoon minced Italian parsley
½	teaspoon pepper
1	turkey, 16 to 18 pounds (7.3 to 8.2 kg)

Good for a Crowd

Set aside 4 of the rosemary sprigs; soak remainder in water to cover for 30 minutes. Meanwhile, combine oil, minced rosemary, parsley, and pepper in a small bowl; set aside.

Discard leg truss from turkey. Remove turkey neck and giblets; reserve for other uses. Remove and discard excess fat. Rinse bird inside and out and pat dry. Place 4 reserved rosemary sprigs inside body cavity. Secure skin over cavities with small metal skewers. Tie legs together and twist wing tips under back.

In a charcoal barbecue, place about a quarter of the soaked rosemary sprigs onto mounds of coals. *In a gas barbecue,* put about a quarter of the soaked rosemary sprigs in a foil pan and place under cooking grate on top of heat source in left front corner of barbecue; turn heat to High and preheat for 10 to 15 minutes. Then turn heat to Indirect/Medium. Arrange turkey, breast side up, in center of cooking grate. Brush with oil mixture. Place lid on grill. Cook turkey, adding another quarter of the sprigs every 30 minutes, until an instant-read thermometer inserted in thickest part of thigh (not touching bone) registers 180°F/82°C (2½ to 3 hours; start checking for doneness after 2 hours). If parts of turkey darken excessively before bird is done, loosely cover those areas with foil.

Transfer turkey to a platter. Let stand for 15 minutes before carving.

MAKES 16 TO 18 SERVINGS PLUS LEFTOVERS.

Per ¼ pound (115 g) boneless cooked turkey, based on percentages of white and dark meat found in average turkey (including skin): 230 calories (42% from fat), 10 g total fat (3 g saturated fat), 93 mg cholesterol, 82 mg sodium, 0 g carbohydrates, 0 g fiber, 32 g protein, 34 mg calcium, 2 mg iron

Grilled Game Hens

Whole grilled hens, coated with a buttery mustard crust, make the centerpiece of a fine meal. To make the game hens cook faster, you can cut them along one side of the backbone before grilling, pull them open, and press them flat.

Charcoal	Indirect
Gas	Indirect/Medium Heat
Grilling time	45–60 minutes

¼ cup (60 ml) butter or margarine, melted

¼ cup (60 ml) Dijon mustard

1 tablespoon minced fresh rosemary or 2 teaspoons crumbled dried rosemary

2 cloves garlic, minced or pressed

4 Rock Cornish game hens, 1¼ to 1½ pounds (565 to 680 g) *each,* thawed if frozen

Rosemary sprigs

Salt and pepper

In a small bowl, combine butter, mustard, minced rosemary, and garlic; set aside.

Remove necks and giblets from game hens; reserve for other uses. Rinse birds inside and out and pat dry. Tie legs together and twist wing tips under back. Coat hens all over with mustard mixture.

Arrange birds, breast side up, in center of cooking grate. Place lid on grill. Cook until meat near thighbone is no longer pink (45 to 60 minutes; cut to test). Transfer to a platter and garnish with rosemary sprigs. Season to taste with salt and pepper.

MAKES 4 TO 6 SERVINGS.

Per serving: 598 calories (58% from fat), 37 g total fat (13 g saturated fat), 212 mg cholesterol, 467 mg sodium, 1 g carbohydrates, 0 g fiber, 60 g protein, 43 mg calcium, 3 mg iron

GRILL BY THE BOOK
T I P

Use sprigs of fresh rosemary as a basting brush to impart additional fragrance and flavor to poultry.

There's good reason why poultry, especially turkey, is traditional at many holiday tables: It's nutritious, economical, and easy to prepare. And when turkey is on the menu, the traditional fixings are often right alongside. Here are three—succotash, sweet potatoes, and stuffing—you can make on the grill; the gravy is prepared on your stovetop using the turkey drippings that collect in the drip pan as the turkey grills.

Corn Succotash

Charcoal	Direct
Gas	Indirect/Medium Heat
Grilling time	About 25 minutes

4   medium-size ears corn, husks and silk removed

1   large red bell pepper

2   tablespoons butter or margarine

1   medium-size onion, chopped

1   package, about 10 ounces (285 g), frozen lima beans, thawed

3   tablespoons whipping cream or half and half (optional)

Salt

Arrange corn and bell pepper on cooking grate. Place lid on grill. Cook, turning occasionally, until some corn kernels are lightly browned and remainder are translucent and bell pepper is blistered and slightly charred (10 to 12 minutes for corn, about 25 minutes for bell pepper). Let cool briefly. Cut kernels from cobs, discarding cobs. Peel, stem, and seed bell pepper; chop. Set corn and bell pepper aside.

In a wide frying pan, melt butter over medium heat. Add onion and lima beans and cook, stirring, until onion begins to turn golden (about 10 minutes). Stir in corn, bell pepper, and, if desired, cream. Season to taste with salt. Cover and cook until corn mixture is hot (5 to 10 more minutes).

MAKES 8 TO 10 SERVINGS.

Per serving: 121 calories (24% from fat), 3 g total fat (2 g saturated fat), 7 mg cholesterol, 55 mg sodium, 21 g carbohydrates, 4 g fiber, 4 g protein, 14 mg calcium, 1 mg iron

Grilled Sweet Potato Slices

Charcoal	Direct
Gas	Indirect/Medium Heat
Grilling time	10–13 minutes

4   medium-size sweet potatoes, sliced ¾ inch (2 cm) thick

½   cup (120 ml) butter or margarine, melted

3   tablespoons firmly packed brown sugar

1   teaspoon ground cinnamon

In a 3- to 4-quart (2.8- to 3.8-liter) pan, bring 2 quarts (1.9 liters) water to a boil. Add potatoes and return water to a boil; reduce heat, cover, and simmer until potatoes are almost tender when pierced (6 to 8 minutes). Let cool briefly; then peel.

In a small bowl, combine butter, brown sugar, and cinnamon. Brush butter mixture all over potatoes. Arrange potatoes on cooking grate. Place lid on grill. Cook, turning once halfway through cooking time, until potatoes are lightly browned (10 to 13 minutes).

MAKES 6 TO 8 SERVINGS.

Per serving: 275 calories (43% from fat), 14 g total fat (8 g saturated fat), 35 mg cholesterol, 153 mg sodium, 37 g carbohydrates, 4 g fiber, 2 g protein, 41 mg calcium, 1 mg iron

Very Easy

Bread Stuffing with Chard & Sausages

Charcoal	Indirect
Gas	Indirect/Medium Heat
Grilling time	About 25 minutes

¼	cup (60 ml) butter or margarine
1	pound (455 g) pork sausages
1¼	cups (300 ml) chopped celery
1	large onion, chopped
4	ounces (115 g) mushrooms, sliced
1½	pounds (680 g) Swiss chard or spinach, finely chopped
1½	teaspoons dried sage
1	teaspoon dried thyme
8	ounces (230 g) sweet French or sourdough bread, cut into ¾-inch (2-cm) cubes
1	cup (240 ml) dry white wine

In a 5- to 6-quart (5- to 6-liter) pan, melt butter over medium-high heat. Add sausages and cook, stirring, until browned (about 10 minutes). Using a slotted spoon, remove sausages and place in a large bowl.

Place celery and onion in pan. Cook, stirring, until vegetables are soft (about 5 minutes). Using a slotted spoon, remove vegetables and add to sausages.

Add mushrooms to pan and cook, stirring, until liquid has evaporated and mushrooms are lightly browned (about 7 minutes). Using a slotted spoon, remove mushrooms and add to sausages.

Add chard to pan and cook, stirring, until chard is wilted and juices have evaporated. Stir chard, sage, thyme, bread cubes, and wine into sausage mixture. Place stuffing in a greased 9-inch (23-cm) square metal pan. Set pan in center of cooking grate. Place lid on grill. Cook until stuffing is lightly browned on top (about 25 minutes).

MAKES 8 TO 10 SERVINGS.

Per serving: 377 calories (67% from fat), 27 g total fat (11 g saturated fat), 48 mg cholesterol, 720 mg sodium, 20 g carbohydrates, 2 g fiber, 10 g protein, 88 mg calcium, 3 mg iron

Good for a Crowd

Turkey Gravy with White Wine

	Giblets and neck from a 10- to 14-pound (4.5- to 6.4-kg) turkey
1	large onion, quartered
1	large stalk celery, chopped
2	bay leaves
½	teaspoon dried thyme
5	cups (1.2 liters) chicken broth
½	cup (120 ml) cornstarch
1	cup (240 ml) dry white wine or chicken broth

Remove liver from giblets; wrap and refrigerate. Combine neck, remaining giblets, onion, celery, bay leaves, thyme, and the 5 cups (1.2 liters) broth in a 3- to 4-quart (2.8- to 3.8-liter) pan. Bring to a boil over high heat; reduce heat, cover, and simmer until giblets are very tender when pierced (about 2¼ hours).

Add liver to pan; cover and simmer for 15 more minutes. Pour broth through a fine strainer into glass measures; discard vegetables and giblets. You should have 5 cups (1.2 liters) broth. If not, return broth to pan and boil over high heat, uncovered, to reduce; or add water to increase and return broth to pan. Set aside.

Pour fat and drippings from turkey into a glass measure. Let stand until fat rises; discard all but ¼ cup (60 ml) of the fat. Add reserved fat and drippings to drip pan. Pour in 1 cup (240 ml) of the broth and cook over medium-high heat, stirring to free browned bits. Scrape mixture into pan with broth.

In a small bowl, stir cornstarch and wine until smooth; add to broth. Cook over high heat, stirring, until mixture comes to a boil. Pour into a gravy boat or a bowl.

MAKES ABOUT 6 CUPS (1.4 LITERS).

Per serving: 126 calories (63% from fat), 8 g total fat (2 g saturated fat), 7 mg cholesterol, 66 mg sodium, 8 g carbohydrates, 1 g fiber, 3 g protein, 12 mg calcium, 0 mg iron

Game Hens in Balsamic Marinade

Butterflied Rock Cornish game hens grill together with skewers of colorful marinated vegetables, making this an easy and elegant entrée to prepare.

Charcoal	Indirect
Gas	Indirect/Medium Heat Searing (optional) see page 6
Marinating time	1 hour or until next day
Grilling time	35–45 minutes

Balsamic Marinade
(see below)

4 Rock Cornish game hens,
1¼ to 1½ pounds (565 to
680 g) *each,* thawed if
frozen

2 medium-size zucchini,
sliced diagonally ½ inch
(1 cm) thick

2 medium-size crookneck
squash, sliced diagonally
½ inch (1 cm) thick

1 large red bell pepper, cut
into 1½-inch (3.5-cm)
squares

8 large mushrooms

8 large shallots

Salt

Balsamic Marinade

⅔ cup (160 ml) balsamic
or red wine vinegar

2 tablespoons Dijon mustard

1 tablespoon minced parsley

1 tablespoon fresh thyme
or 1 teaspoon dried thyme

¼ teaspoon pepper

In a small bowl, combine ingredients for Balsamic Marinade; set aside.

Remove necks and giblets from game hens; reserve for other uses. With poultry or kitchen shears, split each hen lengthwise along one side of backbone. Place birds, skin side up, on a flat surface, pull open, and press firmly, cracking bones slightly, until birds lie reasonably flat. Rinse and pat dry. Place in a large heavy-duty plastic food bag. Put zucchini, crookneck, bell pepper, mushrooms, and shallots in another bag. Pour half the marinade into each bag and seal securely. Rotate bags to distribute marinade and place in a shallow pan. Refrigerate for at least 1 hour or until next day, turning food occasionally.

Remove birds and vegetables from bags and drain, discarding marinade. Using 2 metal skewers at least 15 inches (38 cm) long, thread 2 hens from wing to wing and from thigh to thigh to hold them flat. Repeat for remaining 2 birds, using 2 more skewers. Thread each vegetable separately on 5 more skewers. Arrange birds in center of cooking grate. Arrange vegetables around birds. Place lid on grill. Cook, turning vegetables once halfway through cooking time, until meat near thighbone is no longer pink and vegetables are soft when pressed (35 to 45 minutes; cut hens to test). Season to taste with salt.

MAKES 4 TO 6 SERVINGS.

Per serving: 556 calories (45% from fat), 27 g total fat (7 g saturated fat), 172 mg cholesterol, 317 mg sodium, 18 g carbohydrates, 2 g fiber, 58 g protein, 81 mg calcium, 5 mg iron

Tea-smoked Game Hens

These game hens are served in the manner of Peking duck: thinly sliced and folded into tortillas with green onions, cilantro, and, if you like, hoisin sauce. Warm the tortillas separately so they don't pick up the smoky flavor of the hens.

Charcoal	Indirect
Gas	Indirect/Medium Heat Searing (optional) see page 6
Marinating time	10 minutes or until next day
Grilling time	35–45 minutes

4   Rock Cornish game hens, 1½ to 2 pounds (680 to 905 g) *each*, thawed if frozen

⅓   cup (80 ml) dry sherry

1   teaspoon salt

½   teaspoon ground white pepper

Pared zest from 1 large orange

1   cup (240 ml) fruitwood or mesquite wood chips

½   cup (120 ml) loose black tea leaves

2   star anise or 1 teaspoon anise seeds

2   cinnamon sticks, *each* about 3 inches (8 cm) long

16   green onions

Cilantro sprigs

16   warm flour tortillas, *each* 6 to 7 inches (15 to 18 cm) in diameter

Hoisin sauce (optional)

Remove necks and giblets from game hens; reserve for other uses. With poultry or kitchen shears, cut hens in half. Rinse and pat dry. In a small bowl, combine sherry, salt, and pepper. Brush all over hens. Cover and refrigerate for at least 10 minutes or until next day.

Cut zest into 1-inch (2.5-cm) pieces and place in a large bowl. Add 3 cups (710 ml) water, wood chips, tea, anise, and cinnamon. Cover and let stand for 30 minutes. Pour into a fine strainer set over another bowl; set liquid aside. Transfer wood chip mixture to a foil pan about 4 by 8 inches (10 by 20 cm).

In a charcoal barbecue, set pan on a mound of coals. *In a gas barbecue,* set pan under cooking grate on top of heat source in left front corner of barbecue; turn heat to high and preheat for 10 to 15 minutes. Then turn heat to Indirect/Medium. Arrange hens, skin side down, in center of cooking grate. Place lid on grill. Cook until meat near thighbone is no longer pink (35 to 45 minutes; cut to test).

Transfer hens to a platter. Garnish with onions and cilantro. To serve, slice skin and meat from birds, place in tortillas, and, if desired, season with hoisin sauce. Top with onions and cilantro and fold to enclose filling.

MAKES 8 SERVINGS.

Per serving: 559 calories (44% from fat), 27 g total fat (7 g saturated fat), 154 mg cholesterol, 615 mg sodium, 25 g carbohydrates, 2 g fiber, 52 g protein, 101 mg calcium, 4 mg iron

Asian-spiced Hens with Mango

Cornish game hens marinated in a robust mixture of soy sauce, garlic, ginger, juniper berries, and orange zest are sprinkled with aromatic spices before grilling. Served with mango, orange slices, raspberries, and salad greens, the hens make an inviting and refreshing meal.

Charcoal	Indirect
Gas	Indirect/Medium Heat Searing (optional) see page 6
Marinating time	4 hours or until next day
Grilling time	35–45 minutes

2	Rock Cornish game hens, about 1½ pounds (680 g) *each*, thawed if frozen
	Soy Marinade (see below)
2	large firm-ripe mangoes
2	medium-size oranges
1	tablespoon *each* ground coriander and Chinese five-spice
¼	teaspoon *each* salt and pepper
¼	cup (60 ml) balsamic vinegar
1	tablespoon *each* olive oil and Dijon mustard
4	cups frisée or other greens, rinsed and crisped
6	cups bite-size pieces butter lettuce, rinsed and crisped
½	cup (120 ml) raspberries

Soy Marinade

½	cup (120 ml) soy sauce
¼	cup (60 ml) olive oil
1	tablespoon *each* minced garlic, minced fresh ginger, crushed juniper berries, and grated orange zest

Remove necks and giblets from game hens; reserve for other uses. With poultry shears or a knife, cut birds in half. Rinse and pat dry.

Combine ingredients for Soy Marinade in a large heavy-duty plastic food bag. Add hens and seal bag securely. Rotate bag to distribute marinade and place in a shallow pan. Refrigerate for at least 4 hours or until next day, turning bag occasionally. Meanwhile, peel mangoes. Slice lengthwise down each side of pit, cutting fruit free (you should have 2 rounded cheeks from each). Trim remaining flesh from pits; dice and set aside. Cut peel and white membrane from oranges; slice each crosswise into 6 rounds. Cover and refrigerate fruit.

In a small bowl, combine coriander, five-spice, salt, and pepper. Remove hens from bag and drain, reserving marinade. Pat spice mixture all over hens and mango cheeks. Arrange hens, skin side up, in center of cooking grate. Place lid on grill. Cook for 20 minutes. Place mango cheeks beside birds and continue to cook, brushing food once with reserved marinade halfway through remaining cooking time, until meat near thighbone is no longer pink (15 to 25 more minutes; cut to test).

Meanwhile, stir together reserved diced mango, vinegar, oil, and mustard in a small bowl. Place frisée and lettuce in a bowl and pour dressing over greens; mix lightly. Arrange on a platter or individual plates. With mangoes cut side down, cut fruit into slices ⅜ inch (9 mm) wide, starting ½ inch (1 cm) from top. Place on greens, fanning slices apart. Add oranges and hens. Sprinkle with raspberries.

Makes 4 servings.

Per serving: 712 calories (48% from fat), 38 g total fat (8 g saturated fat), 132 mg cholesterol, 2420 mg sodium, 48 g carbohydrates, 6 g fiber, 46 g protein, 121 mg calcium, 4 mg iron

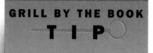

GRILL BY THE BOOK
T I P

To cut fleshy "cheeks" from mango, first locate the wide, flat pit (it runs the length of the fruit). With a sharp knife, peel skin, then cut through mango lengthwise down side of pit until cheek is completely cut off; repeat on other side.

Duck in Citrus-Herb Marinade

A brandy-laced marinade, flavored with lemon, orange, and a garden assortment of fresh herbs, renders these grilled ducks a worthy dinner for special friends.

Charcoal	Indirect
Gas	Indirect/Medium Heat
Marinating time	6 hours or until next day
Grilling time	1½–2 hours

Citrus-Herb Marinade
(see below)

2 ducks, 4 to 5 pounds (1.8 to 2.3 kg) *each,* thawed if frozen

1 or 2 medium-size oranges

2 limes, cut into wedges

Salt and pepper

Citrus-Herb Marinade

½ cup (120 ml) brandy or chicken broth

1 teaspoon *each* grated orange zest and lemon zest

¼ cup (60 ml) *each* orange juice and lemon juice

3 tablespoons *each* Dijon mustard and extra-virgin olive oil

2 cloves garlic, minced or pressed

½ teaspoon ground pepper

1 tablespoon chopped fresh sage or 1 teaspoon dried sage

1 tablespoon chopped fresh rosemary or 1 teaspoon crumbled dried rosemary

1 tablespoon chopped fresh thyme or 1 teaspoon dried thyme

1 tablespoon chopped fresh savory or 1 teaspoon dried savory

In a small bowl, combine ingredients for Citrus-Herb Marinade; set aside.

Remove necks and giblets from ducks; reserve for other uses. Remove and discard excess fat. Rinse ducks inside and out and pat dry. Prick skin all over with a fork. Place each bird in a large heavy-duty plastic food bag. Pour half the marinade into each bag and seal securely. Rotate bags to distribute marinade and place in a shallow pan. Refrigerate for at least 6 hours or until next day, turning bags occasionally.

Remove ducks from bags and drain, reserving marinade. Secure skin over cavities with small metal skewers. Tie legs together and twist wing tips under back.

Arrange ducks, breast side up, in center of cooking grate. Place lid on grill. Cook, brushing occasionally with reserved marinade, until an instant-read thermometer inserted in thickest part of thigh (not touching bone) registers 180°F/82°C (1½ to 2 hours). Meanwhile, cut peel and white membrane from orange; thinly slice crosswise.

Transfer birds to a platter. Garnish with orange slices and lime wedges. Season to taste with salt and pepper.

MAKES 6 SERVINGS.

Per serving: 977 calories (75% from fat), 81 g total fat (26 g saturated fat), 217 mg cholesterol, 336 mg sodium, 10 g carbohydrates, 1 g fiber, 50 g protein, 73 mg calcium, 8 mg iron

Ducks with Soy Sauce

More tender and predictable in flavor, farm-raised ducks offer the added advantage of year-round availability. Be aware, however, that you may have to order them well in advance from your meat market.

Charcoal	Indirect
Gas	Indirect/Medium Heat Searing (optional) see page 6
Marinating time	30 minutes or until next day
Grilling time	30–35 minutes

4 wild or farm-raised mallard ducks, about 2 pounds (905 g) *each*

3 cloves garlic, minced or pressed

¾ cup (180 ml) reduced-sodium soy sauce

¼ teaspoon crushed red pepper flakes

2 lemons, cut into wedges

½ cup (120 ml) canned lingonberries or cranberries

About 2 cups (470 ml) watercress, rinsed and crisped

With poultry shears or a knife, cut ducks in half. Rinse and pat dry. Prick skin all over with a fork.

Combine garlic, soy sauce, and red pepper flakes in a large heavy-duty plastic food bag. Add ducks and seal bag securely. Rotate bag to distribute marinade and place in a shallow pan. Refrigerate for at least 30 minutes or until next day, turning bag occasionally.

Remove ducks from bag and drain, reserving marinade. Arrange birds, bone side down, in center of cooking grate. Place lid on grill. Cook, brushing once with reserved marinade halfway through cooking time, until an instant-read thermometer inserted in thickest part of thigh (not touching bone) registers 180°F/82°C (30 to 35 minutes).

Transfer ducks to a platter or individual plates. Garnish with lemon wedges, lingonberries, and watercress.

MAKES 8 SERVINGS.

Per serving: 599 calories (74% from fat), 49 g total fat (17 g saturated fat),145 mg cholesterol, 562 mg sodium, 5 g carbohydrates, 0 g fiber, 34 g protein, 49 mg calcium, 5 mg iron

Pheasant with Grapes & Orange Sauce

For simple elegance when company is coming, grill pheasants and serve them with a sweet and fruity sauce. You can make the orange sauce a day in advance, if you like, so there will be little left to do but grill the pheasants.

Charcoal	Indirect
Gas	Indirect/Medium Heat
Grilling time	40–45 minutes

Orange Sauce (see below)

2	pheasants, 2 to 2½ pounds (905g to 1.15 kg) *each*
1	small orange
2	teaspoons butter or margarine
3	to 4 cups (710 to 950 ml) stemmed seedless green grapes
	Salt

Orange Sauce

2	large oranges
1½	cups (360 ml) orange juice
½	cup (120 ml) orange-flavored liqueur
3	tablespoons sugar
2	tablespoons Dijon mustard
1	tablespoon currant or raspberry jelly
1	tablespoon brandy

To prepare Orange Sauce, use a vegetable peeler to pare zest (orange part only) from large oranges. Cut zest into thin slivers and place in a 3- to 4-quart (2.8- to 3.8-liter) pan. Cover generously with water and bring to a boil over high heat; drain. Return zest to pan and add 1 cup (240 ml) of the orange juice, liqueur, and sugar. Boil over high heat, stirring, until liquid has almost evaporated (10 to 15 minutes; watch carefully to avoid scorching). Spoon out and set aside 2 tablespoons of the zest.

To pan, add remaining orange juice, mustard, jelly, and brandy. Cook over medium heat, stirring often, until jelly is melted. If made ahead, let cool; then cover and refrigerate sauce and reserved zest separately for up to 1 day.

Remove necks and giblets from birds; reserve for other uses. Remove and discard excess fat. Rinse birds inside and out and pat dry. Cut orange in half; place a half in body cavity of each bird. Secure skin over cavities with small metal skewers. Tie legs together and twist wing tips under back.

Pour 1 cup (240 ml) water into drip pan. Arrange pheasants, breast side down, in center of cooking grate. Place lid on grill. Cook until an instant-read thermometer inserted in thickest part of thigh (not touching bone) registers 180°F/82°C (40 to 45 minutes).

Tilt birds to drain juices into pan. Transfer birds to a platter and let stand for at least 10 minutes before carving. Meanwhile, skim and discard fat from drippings; add drippings to sauce and boil over high heat, stirring, until reduced to about 1 cup (240 ml). Melt butter in a wide frying pan over high heat. Swirl grapes in pan until slightly brighter green and hot (about 3 minutes). Scatter grapes around pheasants; sprinkle birds with reserved zest. Serve with sauce. Season to taste with salt.

MAKES 4 TO 8 SERVINGS.

Per serving: 711 calories (38% from fat), 29 g total fat (8 g saturated fat), 254 mg sodium, 40 g carbohydrates, 2 g fiber, 68 g protein, 60 mg calcium, 4 mg iron

GRILL BY THE BOOK TIP

If drippings are used to prepare a sauce, wear an insulated mitt and use long tongs to lift the drip pan from the grill.

Index